BORROWED TIME

Borrowed Time

A Soldier's Reflection on Finding Yourself Through Chaos

Hien (HT) Tran

Published by Game Changer Publishing

Paperback ISBN: 978-1-965653-89-0

Hardcover ISBN: 978-1-965653-84-5

Digital ISBN: 978-1-965653-85-2

www.GameChangerPublishing.com

DEDICATION

This book is dedicated to my father, Hieu Tran, who has made many sacrifices in his life to ensure that his sons would have the opportunity to succeed in life. A selfless, giving man who has never asked for anything more than our best efforts.

I would also like to dedicate this moment to my brothers of the 2nd Battalion 22nd Infantry Anvil Company 1st Platoon of the 10th Mountain Division. With God's grace, thank you for saving my life. I am doing this for us because your efforts to save me through the night will not be wasted in this lifetime. There are more mountains to conquer... with every last breath.

I would like to take a moment to thank my incredible wife, Nadine Tran, and my amazing kiddos, Clayton and Annabelle Tran, for always believing in me. You guys are the greatest blessings in my life.

All the glory belongs to GOD… without His Love and Blessings, I am nothing.

"DEEDS NOT WORDS,"

"CLIMB TO GLORY" - 2-22 INF, 10th Mountain Division

READ THIS FIRST

Just to say thanks for buying and reading my book,
I would like to connect!

Scan the QR Code Here:

SCAN ME

BORROWED TIME

A SOLDIER'S REFLECTION ON FINDING
YOURSELF THROUGH CHAOS

HIEN (HT) TRAN

CONTENTS

FOREWORD

We met HT when he was working with our son Patrick at a local Macy's. One day he asked several questions regarding our faith. Eventually, it led to his conversion. We celebrated his Baptism with much joy! HT struggled to identify a path for his life. He shared with us that he felt serving his country would offer him an opportunity to give back to America. He served with the Army in Iraq and was wounded in combat. He lost an eye and had a leg injury. We were very blessed to be with him at the Walter Reed Hospital. We brought him many cards and letters from our Saint Anthony parish. It was one of the most memorable and sad times for us.

Thankfully, he recovered and met a beautiful woman (Dee) who would become his wife. They have two wonderful children. HT started a small construction business called Anvil Builders Inc. to support Veterans, a company named after his Infantry unit that he served with. He continues to foster veteran's programs, lending his voice and support to multiple organizations. God spared HT so he could come back to be on a journey with Him. He is a man with so much humility and love. There are many who are the recipients of his generosity, faith and compassion.

We are so very proud of our Warrior Godson!
Beverly and Pat Nocero

INTRODUCTION

"Stop being the best for the world, be the best that you can be..."
–Brene Brown

The night was clear as dust settled around my team and me. We had just been dropped off on our objective on May 10, 2008, in a classified area in Iraq after a rough landing from the Chinook that transported us. Life is funny that way: We can plan all we want, but things rarely go the way we need them to. I suppose that's the theme of my life; the path has never been easy, though I have no one to blame but myself. As we gathered ourselves, I noticed a house flicker its lights. We all knew what that meant: They knew we were here. My platoon knew it was about to go down, and we had to reach that house as fast as we could.

Life is full of unexpected moments, but you never know how big a moment will be. We think we're ready, but sometimes, things don't play out in our favor. After much planning and discussion, we moved as one, and then I saw a bright blast and felt sand and dirt hit my face. At that instant, all our lives changed forever. As I gasped for air, I heard voices calling out to me. There was a figure in front of me, but I couldn't make out who or what it was. My face was numb; I couldn't feel it or move my body, and a burning sensation flushed over me. Lying there, none of the materialistic sh*t in my life mattered—not one cent. I was just trying to hold on to memories of my loved ones, knowing this could be my last moment. That moment stretched like an eternity, though it was only seconds. I clung to those memories for dear life, but everything started to dim, and then there was darkness.

However, that wasn't the moment that changed my life—it was just one that redefined it. My true turning point came with a question that shifted my entire perspective on life itself: "If you were to die today, what would people say about you?" This is not about war stories, this is a book on the war I have waged with myself trying to define who I am. I am also not the hero of this book.

So...Who am I? Today, I am a husband, father, veteran, entrepreneur, advocate, leader, and a new author. But at the core, I am just a man who's taken a long journey and learned many hard lessons. Strip away all those titles, and I'm just like you. I've worked hard to earn those titles, but they don't define me; they're simply facets of who I am. I've evolved, and with each evolution, I've had to fight through expectations and perceptions to reach where I am today. My biggest obstacle has always been myself, and I'm not always proud of the person I see in the mirror. Doubts, insecurities, and mistakes have led me to my own share of hardship. Quitting was easier than fighting through pain and misery. But sometimes, you have to hit rock bottom to truly find yourself. That is where the fight matters the most. There's only one way out, and it starts with you.

We often let ourselves be handcuffed by others' perceptions and expectations, carrying that weight until it breaks us and we lose sight of who we are. When that happens, we walk around like victims, that life dealt us a bad hand... even though we let it happen. It's time to change that and face the fight. It's not about winning or losing; it's about enduring all 12 rounds. The result is for everyone else watching; the real question is, "Did I give it all my effort?" Because once you step out of the ring, it is final.

I'm not writing this book because I have everything figured out. I'm far from it, and I'm still learning about myself every day. I'm better at embracing the highs and lows in life, and I no longer run from them; I prepare for them. My faith in God and His trust in me help me push through. The difference between you and me is that I've been blessed with a second chance at life. This is my "Borrowed Time." This isn't about wealth, because money only matters to those who don't yet understand the value of life. My purpose has changed. I'm writing this book to impact one person's life. If you're reading this and you're feeling mentally and spiritually empty, whatever situation you're facing, no matter how overwhelming it feels, know you're not alone. Keep fighting and swinging. I promise—it'll be worth it because you matter. I'll walk with you, friend, because we all need someone to be by our side to believe in us. I had a whole community behind me on my journey… I can be a part of yours.

I've seen too many losses to count, more than enough to fill the world with goodbyes and sorrows. I hope that by the time you reach the end of this book, you'll feel inspired to find yourself, your purpose, and continue to appreciate your journey. We all grow in different ways, but accountability and responsibility rest with you and the choices you make.

We will start with my journey and reflect on where I started and where I am now. Let's begin by breaking free from the expectations and perceptions that have held you back. Only you can define who you are and who you're meant to be.

"If you let people's perception of you indicate you as a person, you will never grow as a person."
–Mr. Feeny (*Boy Meets World*)

CHAPTER 1

"Being a man is what you make it. You can't always
live up to expectations. You try to please everybody while
you struggle, so you fake it and end up out of balance."
–"To Be a Man," by Dax featuring Darius Rucker

The definition of expectation is "a strong belief that something will happen or will be the case in the future," according to Google. These presumptions are placed upon us from the moment we're born into this world. As a man, I believe there are countless expectations imposed on us from boyhood to manhood, and often, these expectations serve others rather than ourselves. This is the story of my life and how I finally came to understand those "expectations." I can only share my perspective as a man and how I have become who I am today.

As I get older, I look back on these expectations and feel the weight of the responsibility I carried, which shaped who I am and how I respond to life. Did I meet the standard or fall short? Am I staying true to the man I need to be, or am I merely the man others want me to be? These questions have many layers, and it wasn't always easy to understand or recognize them in each moment. Now, as I approach my late 40s, I see more clearly, blessed with a second chance at life and a new perspective. It's always been a challenge for me to reconcile the man I am inside with the image I present to the world. Expectations are layered deeply within my heritage, culture, society, religion, and most importantly, within myself.

Growing up as a first-generation Vietnamese American in San Jose, CA, came with its own struggles. Publicly, I was just an American kid, but at home, I was a traditional Vietnamese son. I wanted to be myself, but just being me wasn't enough—there were responsibilities, duties, and obligations I had to fulfill. This wasn't something I knew how to navigate or separate as I evolved into adulthood. What does it mean to be a man? I've been asking myself this question my whole life, often equating it to a set of rules and standards I had to meet to be considered one. I think these days, the expectation of being a man weighs so heavily that it's either make or break. One of my biggest fears has always been falling short of that expectation.

I was born in '79 and raised in the '80s and '90s, so my understanding of manhood is rooted in old-school values. A man is supposed to do certain things, but above all, he must provide for his family, doing whatever it takes to make that happen. My dad was a prime example of this for me. Manhood meant adhering to cultural, societal, and religious expectations, while my own self-expectations always seemed to come last. For a long time, I didn't know if my own expectations even mattered. I'm not blaming anyone for this, but everyone else's perceptions and expectations often took priority over my own, and I struggled with that. I didn't fully confront it until later in life when I had to look myself in the mirror and redefine who I wanted to be. Eventually, enough was enough.

I've gone through countless evolutions of myself, filled with both good and bad moments, and I'm appreciative of the journey that has brought me to who I am today. The expectations I carry now are no longer those of others—they are my own. Realizing this has been one of life's greatest lessons for me.

Culturally, growing up Vietnamese American was like a bootcamp in itself. My parents held very strong expectations. Education was the highest priority, and grades always had to be above par (meeting par wasn't even an option—my fellow Asian-heritage readers can probably relate to that).

Getting a "B" was tolerated, but always questioned: What more could I have done to get an "A"? To me, an "A" was as close as I could get to being the perfect kid in my parents' eyes, academically speaking. It was exhausting because I knew I couldn't maintain it forever. As a Vietnamese American kid, school felt endless, and though I didn't enjoy it, I wanted to make my parents proud. They sacrificed so much and left even more behind before coming to the United States. They lost their home country and left their families to give themselves a chance at a better life after enduring a war-torn homeland where they didn't agree with the principles or the way of life. They had to start over from scratch, so these expectations weren't just ideals; they were goals for building a new life and creating a future. This opportunity couldn't be wasted.

Change does not come easily for the Tran family. But when my dad made it to America and had me, he had to shift his priorities and expectations to raise me. My dad is a good, hard-working man, my example of what a man should be for his family. As a kid, I never quite understood his purpose or what he was trying to accomplish. I consider him brave; he always put my brother and me before himself, though he made it clear what he expected of us. We were to succeed in our education to build good careers and not waste the opportunity he had sacrificed so much to provide. But to be honest, that didn't fully align with the American values I was being raised with in school. This gap in perspective and communication between us created a lot of tension because being "cool" and accepted by my peers was more important to me than always being a good student. My dad didn't understand the struggles I faced internally, feeling like I didn't fully belong at school. What I saw outside our home didn't match how things were inside. I didn't share the same values and mindset as my peers, nor did I have the same level of "freedom."

The Tran family held high standards, especially around education. From the start, we weren't on the same cultural level —the American way versus the Vietnamese way of doing things. I felt so conflicted by it all; I was like a double agent. Sorting through it all as an adolescent felt overwhelming. (I was drowning in silence.) I remember that from a very young age, we weren't allowed to speak English at home; only Vietnamese was permitted. In public, I was always asked to translate for my dad, which embarrassed me deeply. I wanted to be seen as an American, as equal to my friends, instead of being marked as an outsider with "slanted eyes." I fought hard for that, and nothing was worse than being called "Charlie"—a term I didn't even understand at the time.

Having to translate in public felt like a huge burden, especially because I was insecure about whether I was translating correctly. But more than that, it was about perception. I convinced myself that speaking Vietnamese in public made me less "American," making me feel like I wouldn't be accepted. Knowing I had these internal conflicts, I tried hard to be a good son and succeed in school, because I knew it mattered to my dad. I love him with all my heart, and as an adult, I understand the sacrifices he made for us, sacrifices that became the basis of his expectations.

My dad just wanted my brother and me to do better than he did, based on everything he gave up to come to this country. My parents arrived in America with only what they wore on their backs, leaving behind their dreams for the hope of a better future—for me and my brother. We were a low-income family, and my dad worked constantly to provide for us. We didn't function as a typical nuclear family; my dad worked the grave-yard shift and picked up every hour he could to give us what we needed (though rarely what we wanted). My mom did her best with us at home, but the pressure was high. I spent my whole life, until I left for college, trying to make my dad proud. He's a man of few words, but even now, his look of disapproval gives me chills. That's not his fault—it's because I've conditioned myself to seek his approval. It sounds entitled even to admit that, but as a kid, I wasn't mature enough to see it that way. (Simply selfish...) Looking back, I realize I overlooked all his sacrifices just because I wanted acceptance from people who barely knew me.

His only expectation, based on what he sacrificed, was for me to succeed in this American life while holding onto our cultural and traditional values. I was supposed to become an educated man with a solid career. Of course, those careers fell within the "top four:" doctor, lawyer, engineer, or a U.S. Naval Officer. That didn't exactly pan out. (LOL, let's go Army!) I'm considered the black sheep of the family for that decision. But that was our version of the American Dream. My dad sacrificed so much that I had to succeed in life, right?

———

We were taught at a very early age that being an American is a privilege and not a right. Looking back, I realize I had misinterpreted my dad's intentions throughout my journey. I thought I was doing it all for us or for him, but he wanted me to do it for myself. My success would validate everything he had lost, sacrificed, and endured—all represented by his sweat, tears, and hope. He needed my brother and me to understand that his love language was his continued support, even now as adults, because we were his legacy of the American Dream. He wanted us to realize that the American privileges we saw as rights could be taken away in an instant, making them privileges, not guarantees. This was a seed planted from his own reflections and memories of a country, family, and friends he had lost during the Vietnam War.

Growing up in my community, I had different expectations for myself and my friends. Previously, I mentioned feeling like a double agent because the actions and decisions I made didn't always align with house rules (Dad's rules). My friends, who grew up with me on the same street, accepted me for who I was, making me feel like part of a family. Most of my neighborhood friends were Mexican and Black, and many were either in or affiliated with the Crips or Norteños. Me? I had no initiation or commitments—they always saw me as a smart, kind kid and took care of the only Asian kids on PDR Street, South Side of San Jose, for over a decade. My brother and I were lucky to have that backing; no one messed with us, and we defended our street as best as we could—like our "homies" did, or at least tried to. They were always protective of us, just as we were of them.

Later, other Asian families moved in, but I never connected with them because I didn't want to be associated with them—I was trying to escape my home life. Reflecting on this now, I know I was living a lie. No matter what I was doing or the trouble I was heading toward, my dad's voice was always in the back of my mind. I knew right from wrong; I just chose to ignore it at times (#facts). Sure, I'd be "down" for my street and hood, but I always had to think twice about what I was doing to make sure my dad wouldn't find out about the trouble I was getting into. How "down" was that? My friends knew it, too, but they never judged me. We had been together since first grade, and I think we all understood—I was a smart kid making dumb choices, seeking respect. I was also the smallest kid on the block —actually, the smallest kid in grade, middle, high school, and even now in adulthood (cue eye roll). But that never mattered to them.

Some of the older guys, whom I respectfully call OGs, had an interesting conversation with me one day before I left for college. "Hanes," they said—they never quite got my name right —"we know you're down with us, but you can never be us. It's not because we don't love you, but because you can be something more. You're a good kid… a smart kid. When you get your first opportunity to leave here, don't come back. Do better than us. If we'd had what you have, we wouldn't be here either. This is a life choice, and we made ours a long time ago. Make us proud and represent us, but if you come back and we know you failed… that *ss is going to get beat." Those words stayed with me, and I never forgot that encouragement, though it broke my heart at the time.

When I wasn't at home, I was out playing and hanging with the crew. That was my daily escape, my chance to act up without facing repercussions. My love for the streets conflicted deeply with the American Dream I was supposed to build. There, I could just be myself without all the expectations. But as soon as 7 p.m. hit, or the streetlights came on, we'd scatter as if a grenade was about to explode. Now, as I approach 45 this September, I would tell my younger self that I was just a wannabe. It wasn't the life I truly wanted; it was about acceptance, something my friends and I all craved because we felt like the odds were against us from the start. We couldn't envision our potential or see a future we could belong to. It's painful to admit, but at the time, it felt true.

The expectations and pressure of trying to realize my potential felt overwhelming. I knew I couldn't live up to it at the time. At school, I was often underestimated and seen as weak or sensitive, especially when trouble found me. I avoided confrontation, letting people push me around because I feared disappointing my dad more than losing a fight. That inner conflict broke my spirit because the values of these two worlds clashed constantly. By the time I left for college, I felt like I needed a new identity. I went from Hien to HT, yet I still didn't feel "normal." And what does "normal" even mean, right? People have tried to define it for me, but no matter how they tried, I never found a way to define it for myself. I've never truly been comfortable with the word "normal."

I faced a unique struggle: wanting to be American but also wanting to make my dad proud. In high school, I was a great student, but once I tasted freedom in college, everything went downhill. I ignored the "voice" inside and, at one point, even refused to go home after being academically disqualified. I was just carefree to the max and completely disregarded my grades. UC Santa Barbara was my ticket to freedom, but thanks to poor decisions, it didn't last long. Reality eventually came knocking.

For me, working hard in high school meant getting the chance to leave home. I knew that didn't match the cultural expectations my family had, but that goal led me down the wrong path of self-discovery. As a college student, I was far from successful. At one point, I drank heavily to cope and smoked marijuana as a release from the world's pressures. It was a temporary escape from expectations, but it brought a lot of hurt, disappointment, and self-resentment. Wanting to be carefree hurt me, and I knew it hurt my dad. I was over school and what others expected me to be. But this mindset came at a price—a price I couldn't afford.

Tasting freedom made me think this was what life was supposed to be. But when my grades came in, that sense of freedom was validated by a failing GPA of .16 in my first quarter as a freshman. I'll say it, because it's about being accountable: what a dumbass. Smart in high school, but an idiot in college. By the end of my freshman year, I had placed myself on academic disqualification after two probation periods. Instead of rising to the occasion, I dug myself into a hole.

At 18, I became a runner from my problems—a sprinter, really. I blamed the system, others, everyone but myself, for my failures. I refused to put in the work academically and instead worked out constantly, trying to maintain my image. One thing I could say is that I was in great shape because I was always at the gym, just not in my classes. But how far did that really get me? Not far at all.

The pressure grew unbearable. Each day, the lies and excuses I told myself became a mental cancer. I remember one day, half hanging out of my dorm room window on the sixth floor, looking down and thinking, *I can't go home after all the poor choices I've made.* I couldn't lie to my dad anymore; it wouldn't be fair to him after everything he'd done for me. I felt like ending my life was the only escape.

But fate intervened, and I believe God sent me a blessing in the form of a friend, a brother, and a hero: Silas Pompa. He walked in as I was leaning out the window, grabbed me, and I let it all out. The relief was incredible. He knew I was hurting and assured me that I'd be okay. He reminded me this was just a bump in the road and that I'd make more mistakes, but they'd only remain mistakes if I didn't learn from them. I wasn't proud of myself, but with his help, I started to consider how I'd get through this and eventually become a man of my own.

My dad saw one image of me, and the world saw another, but what image was I trying to portray? Eventually, the truth had to come out; it's inevitable. Nature always knows how to restore balance, but for me, that wasn't enough. My cultural expectations led me to feel insecure about meeting societal expectations. Everyone eventually has to grow up and cross that road, and for me, that meant asking, *What does it mean to be an adult, or a man?* Who teaches you to be *the* man? Responsibilities and sacrifices seem endless, like there's an invisible checklist of what you need to accomplish. It freaked me out, but as I looked around, I realized my peers were experiencing the same thing. We were all trying to figure it out alone, which is terrifying because you're walking this path blindly, hoping you're doing it right. There's no manual to guide you. I chuckle now because, as a kid, I thought I'd know exactly what to do at 18. Instead, I kept running into walls, persevering through the bumps and bruises with each decision I made, knowing I had to keep moving forward in hopes of eventually course-correcting.

Ironically, the "expectations" I was hiding from ended up being the landmarks guiding me back on track. I knew I needed to graduate from college, buy a home, and build a career. I didn't need all the details then—I just needed to get there, but I didn't even know where to start.

I found myself wondering if there was some equation where doing X, Y, and Z would yield the results I needed to bring order to my life. Here I was, the one Asian kid who hated math, trying to use algebra to solve life. Ironic, isn't it?

I spent more than half my life trying to figure out my place in society and build a plan I could be proud of. It wasn't easy. Eventually, I had to leave UC Santa Barbara and return home because I no longer had the energy to do it my way. It cost me my pride and ego and nearly my life. I was humbled. When I transferred home, I fixed my grades and started over.

The only reason I graduated from college was that my dad had been waiting almost seven years to see me walk at graduation. I wanted to make him proud, but when the time came… I couldn't bring myself to attend my graduation from San Jose State University. My dad was disappointed, and it broke his heart, but for the first time, I had to be honest with him. To him, that graduation might have validated everyone else's hard work, but to me, it highlighted my failures: My arrogance had left me barely able to scrape by academically. I couldn't face a crowd of people who had earned their moment, while I felt like I was just sliding by. That diploma, something he was proud of because his firstborn had achieved it, felt to me like a mark of disappointment and a scar of having given up on myself. The look on his face is something I'll never forget. I had taken away his moment of pride. There was nothing to celebrate.

The only question left was, *What's next?* I knew I didn't want to pursue any of the things my dad had hoped for. He wasn't wrong to want more for me—I just didn't know what I wanted for myself. Strangely, even from a young age, I had wanted to be in the military. I know it sounds silly. Here I was, desperate to be free, yet drawn to a world of discipline.

This struck a chord in my family's tradition. We come from strong military roots, yet, of my generation of Vietnamese Americans, including my cousins, my brother, and me (about 60 of us across the States), no one had joined. I was fascinated with the military, but not for the right reasons. Looking back, I realize that it was all about the uniform and the "booty." Immaturity played a big role back then, as I was still fixated on that false self-image. But my dad didn't want me to pursue the military; hence, his top four career choices for me—the classic Vietnamese aspirations. He reminded me that he had escaped a war-torn country and came to the United States to ensure we'd never experience war. The only exception was if I became a Naval Officer from Annapolis; that would honor our tradition. Yeah... I definitely wasn't meeting those expectations. (I'd look like a short Stay Puft Marshmallow Man—a *Ghostbusters* reference for my younger readers.)

When it's part of who you are and where you come from, it's hard to ignore it. You feel you have to "give it your best shot," but, to be honest, I was doing it for all the wrong reasons. Even if I had entered the military at a young age (which I didn't), I didn't understand the true meaning of service. To serve, obey, and understand order requires discipline and breaking barriers beyond yourself. I didn't make it because I didn't meet the requirements—not even the minimum or the exception. Serving your country means giving everything for others, and at that stage in my life, I couldn't grasp it. I had all the letters and administrative paperwork, but ultimately, I lacked the physical attributes they wanted. By the grace of God, I was too short (story of my life), but in reality, I wasn't mentally ready either. So, it was time to move along. That's why I took the college route. And, well, we all know how that went.

As you read this, you might think I'm too hard on myself—that I need to chill. But I'm being as honest as I can because I don't want you to think the author of this book had his life together when he didn't. To help you understand my transformation, which I call a "work in progress," I have to share my downfalls. I'm not boasting—I'm holding myself accountable for my actions and decisions. This is part of my journey to reflect, rebuild, and redefine my expectations with honesty. I'm a different person today than I was 20 years ago, and we all are. But you can't appreciate the work you put in until you acknowledge the struggles you went through.

Society sets the standard for what your life should look like: Go to school until you're 18, then choose one of two paths—work or more school. Only those who truly know themselves find a third option, breaking the mold to carve their own path. After that, you often end up with an eight-to-five job (or longer), marriage, starting a family, and then, for the next generation, the cycle repeats. For those of us who build the "right" plan (I use that term loosely), we might eventually retire. Then, age sets in, and we wait for "our moment," and life goes on. So, let me ask again: Between these stages, as a man, what is expected of us? Is it to provide, to conquer our careers, to explore the world—something only a few can afford—or are we just one small cog keeping the world turning? No matter how I answer that question, it sometimes just doesn't feel like enough. There's a void that can't be filled.

As men, we're expected to be protectors, the ones others depend on and lean on. It's our role from birth; we're supposed to be tough. But it's exhausting. Who takes care of us? Who checks in on us? I fear failing to be the man I should be. I searched for guidance, a set of instructions, and was looking in all the wrong places. The example was there all along, but I was too immature to see it—my dad was that example. He was everything I wanted to be. (Love you, Dad.) As I grew older, I began to appreciate the standard he set for us, a standard I had blindly overlooked when I was young.

We used to have Sunday night dinners, and he'd tell us stories about Vietnam, the war, and all he had to do to survive. As an American kid, those stories went in one ear and out the other. "Oh no, my parents are talking again... why?" I've seen other Vietnamese kids grow up deeply connected to their parents and their struggles, but that wasn't me with my dad. (I was a bit aloof and disrespectful on the inside, though outwardly well-behaved.) I always hated the comparisons with how disciplined other kids were or their grades. I couldn't live up to those expectations and felt the weight of them constantly. People would say, "Oh, he's such a good kid, a good young man," but I didn't understand how his stories, his sacrifices, connected to what he wanted from me in that moment.

This affected me on another level, especially in personal relationships. I couldn't commit because I didn't know what anyone wanted from me. If you thought I was a sprinter with cultural and societal expectations, I could've been an Olympic sprinter (not really, just an analogy) when it came to personal relationships. As soon as someone had feelings and focused on me… I was gone. And if I caught feelings first and they acknowledged it… gone again. It was all about the chase, but I couldn't commit. I hurt a lot of people, and I'm not proud of it. I knew that at some point, someone would expect something from me, and I just didn't deal with it. I didn't even try to work around it. Eventually, I just said, "Forget it, I don't want to do this anymore." That attitude ruined a lot of relationships with people I truly cared about. I was so unhappy with myself that I'd either walk away or find an excuse not to commit. I was an a**hole, and it wasn't right to treat women that way. Now, I have a beautiful daughter, and if a boy pulled that sh*t with her… straight-up a** whooping. I'm serious—this is me being honest.

In my life, I've only had two serious relationships that lasted more than a year, and I'm now married to the amazing woman who helped redefine my views on love and expectations. (She's a warrior in her own right; dealing with me isn't easy. I love you, Nadine Tran.)

As a man, you're told to live and learn from *all* the decisions you make. Good or bad, we create our own paths, with no one to blame but ourselves. We have to look inward and understand what we're made of. Some of us have what we need and seek what we don't; others need to seek more and then build on what they have. But it has to be intentional, not just transactional. Checking things off a list feels good, but they need to be things you need to do, not just want to do. Eventually, I realized the expectations I was trying to satisfy were never really my own. That was the turning point in my life: once I understood what I needed out of life, I could verbalize it and manifest it for myself.

But getting there was part of the journey. The end result isn't what matters most; it's the journey itself. It's in the mix of right and wrong decisions where growth happens, and that's my journey to account for. Once I understood that, I stopped caring about what anyone else thought. It took a long time to get there, but it was worth it.

Growing into my thirties, I often joke that if I could go back and talk to my twenty-something self, I'd either shake some sense into that version of HT or start swinging. That's how frustrated I am with my younger self because I know I could have done things better or made wiser choices. But what good is it to dwell on that now? I wish I'd been more graceful, appreciative, and, most importantly, confident in communicating my needs. I spent my teenage years and twenties trying to be someone who didn't fit who I really wanted to be, either by comparing myself to others or wandering aimlessly without a clear purpose. I wasted time by not being intentional and allowing self-created distractions to block my growth. I needed to find meaning in what I was doing as part of the process. I had to build faith in myself to create an impact.

One of my struggles growing up was understanding my faith as a man. Who, what, and where should I place my heart? I was raised in a Buddhist home with many traditions I didn't fully understand or connect with. I was curious about my friends who went to church. I definitely believe in a higher being, but I didn't know how to make it personal. As a kid, faith and belief meant praying to the universe for things I couldn't get. As I grew older, I began questioning my belief system because of certain events in my life as I was trying to mature. Bad experiences made me question where I stood in this world, whether I was big or small in the grand scheme of things. This difference in perspective was, once again, a cultural gap for me. One faith felt more personal in my eyes, while the other was simply following tradition.

As an example of how out of touch my understanding of reverence was, I was raised with certain traditions—Chinese New Year, Moon Festival, ceremonial prayer worship, lunar calendar practices. But to me, these were routines that held very little personal meaning. I knew they were part of my heritage, but I never felt a deep connection to them. They felt transactional, and I don't mean to be disrespectful by saying that. Deep down, I knew I needed a bond, and now, looking back, I see that I was always the problem. I didn't understand my faith; I treated prayer and spirituality as if I had a "genie in a bottle," expecting instant gratification.

My curiosity was piqued when I heard others talk about their relationship with God, as if God was their best friend. The key word there is *relationship*.

When people around me went through hard times, they leaned on a higher being, but I didn't feel I had that. I lacked an intentional relationship because my intentions were probably selfish—it was always about me. I wasn't ready, and that kind of relationship needed time and experiences beyond my control. People say God plants seeds and lets His love grow within you, and when it blossoms, it's the most beautiful experience. I wanted that—a deep, personal relationship with a higher being... my Father, His Son, and the Holy Spirit. I now see how dangerous it can be to walk through life without belief. I've been down that dark road, trying to fill myself with things that seemed to make me happy, only to feel empty at the end of each day.

The worst question to ask yourself is, *Why me?* I know now

that only one being has that answer, and it's not for us to understand but to carry out our purpose once we find that resolve with Him. It's a blind trust and a happiness that can't be explained.

God found me before I enlisted in the Army in 2006. I'm sure you can see how miserable of a person I was then (some might say that's still me). I finally found my purpose, and for the first time, I didn't seek anyone's approval. I converted to Catholicism without my dad's permission, and I was scared. But I stood on my own conviction, inspired by the peace I saw others find with God. These people weren't seeking anything for themselves—they simply wanted peace. They weren't perfect, and life had challenged and even broken some of them, but they kept moving forward because their faith was strong. Their journey wasn't about achieving specific results; it was about learning and understanding the pilgrimage. Like me, they'd made good and bad decisions, but they learned from all of it, not just one or the other. That built meaning, something I'd always felt I lacked. Telling you this doesn't make me holy; it just makes me a believer who feels blessed to still be on this journey. I wanted to stop feeling empty and start feeling "whole" after the void I'd created for myself. I wanted to open my eyes and embrace life's journey with everything it had in store for me.

I've realized that if I can't define my own love, happiness, or expectations, I can't expect others or the world to do it for me. How can I be authentic when all I've done is emulate what I wanted, not what I needed? That's the scary part—being lost without faith. But by truly trusting in Him, He leads you beyond what you thought were your limits.

I believe this also applies to love, especially for men. The complexity of emotions is shaped by the way we're shown to express love. For many men, "love" is a loaded word because we aren't used to hearing it or seeing it expressed in traditionally affectionate ways. Love in my family was expressed through providing and sacrificing, not through verbal affirmation. We didn't say "I love you" to each other; I usually only heard those words on TV shows and movies. Love, as I understood it, was about providing for the family and sacrificing yourself to ensure they had what they needed. I never saw my parents say it to each other or to us, but we were always cared for.

Society and the world often define love as romance, but that's only one part of it. Another part is appreciation, and the rest is the sacrifice you make for others, putting their needs above your own.

True love comes with maturity... which, for a long time, was something I was far from. As an American kid, I sought the words—the Hollywood version of romance that producers placed in front of me. But as soon as I heard those words come from a young woman's mouth, all I could think about was the commitment that was coming. I cracked under the pressure because I knew I'd have to navigate her emotions and feelings, which I had little aptitude for. I'd sprint away from that courtship, never to return.

Love isn't always about intimacy and romance; it's about appreciation as well, within limits. The keyword here is *limit*— too much of anything can turn harmful or breed resentment. The only thing that should be limitless is our love and appreciation for what God has blessed us with. Most men just want to be appreciated as part of love. Often, we seek more because it feels good, but it can quickly become an imbalance and knock us off our feet. There's no easy formula for love, and that was something I struggled with for a long time. Truly understanding its meaning took time and experience.

I remember the first time my dad told me he loved me—it was when I graduated from Ft. Benning, Georgia. I was already overwhelmed with emotion, having made it through 24 weeks of training that tested my limits.

Hearing those words from my dad filled me with joy because I knew he was proud of what I had accomplished. Normally, if you told him you loved him, his automatic response would be to say, "Thank you." I appreciate that, no matter my age, he continues to be there in his own traditional way, rolling out his questions to understand and support me. It's not always enjoyable, but that's his love language. His love language for me was always food and providing for my brother and me. Now, as an adult, I know he has my back no matter what, but as a child, I often tried to escape his care because I misunderstood his intentions. As he ages, I realize I have a limited time to appreciate this love because of all the time I wasted not trying to relate to him. For a man, appreciation goes a long way, recharging him to keep going for those he loves. My dad was a prime example of that.

Another essential part of love is sacrifice. This is something I've watched my dad do for my brother and me since we were babies, and he continues to do so for us as adults. He never does anything for himself, and now, as a father of two, I finally understand it. The realization came almost instantly—I knew that if I were going to emulate anything as a father, it would be my dad's selflessness.

As I redefined my own expectations of manhood, I began to reshape my ideas of what kind of husband and father I wanted to be. I wanted to be a man who loves, supports, provides for, and protects his family. Suddenly, I found common ground with my dad's perspective. After years of complaining, comparing, and feeling misunderstood, I could empathize with him. "You do what it takes..." A man is happy to carry the load for his family, no matter how heavy it is; he bears it alone, and the reward is the smile and peace he creates for his loved ones. A man embraces it all... but who checks on him? Often, no one does, because he doesn't reveal his struggles or exhaustion; he keeps them hidden to ensure others' happiness. We may see glimpses, but never the full weight. Society doesn't see men as nurturers or expect them to admit to nurturing, but this is often the reality we live in—struggling in silence.

The older I get, the more I find myself balancing and understanding the small lessons my dad was trying to teach me. I return to his cultural expectations: he was raising an American boy with Vietnamese heritage. His approach was traditional, while I wanted to embrace the modern, American way. He held onto an old world to safeguard his child's future. I was the connection between the past he remembered and the future he hoped for, adapting as best he could—something I never gave him credit for until I became a parent myself. He escaped his homeland for a new place; I was born here in comfort, while he remembered hardship. Our perspectives clashed because I wanted the American way, and he held to the Vietnamese way. I didn't see or understand this bigger picture until I got married and became a parent.

The rolling tide of questions and expectations surged within me because now, it was about more than just myself. *What am I supposed to do now? How do I provide for and support my family?* And then, becoming a father raised even more questions: *What kind of father do I need to be, and how am I going to do this?* I kept thinking that the father I become will shape the man my son grows into. As parents, we always want to do what's right for our children, often setting our needs aside... and then everything came full circle.

My dad had always sacrificed his dreams, his career, and his time to ensure we had what we needed. He made it seem so effortless because he never talked about it; he just did what was necessary. Realizing this as I transitioned into fatherhood myself stirred up feelings of regret that I hadn't understood it sooner. I felt a deep sense of anguish.

Expressing my feelings is a new experience for me. Friends and family often joke that anger was my only recognizable emotion. Anger kept me going, serving as my tool to prove people wrong. It sparked the stubbornness I needed to push through when others doubted me. I'm not saying this to boast; I'm sharing it to highlight a weakness I've identified in myself. I used to do things for others' approval rather than my own. Silence, silence... and then KABOOM. It wasn't a good look. But now, I don't care what people think. I've come to value myself and appreciate my journey, realizing that it only matters what my family and I think. It's a peaceful place to be, free from the exhaustion of others' opinions.

This realization changed my outlook and perspective. I'm now comfortable as a man expressing vulnerability and talking about my feelings—not to burden others, but to connect and support them. It's a bit taboo for me because, at times, sharing emotions is perceived as weakness. Society imposes an image we're expected to uphold, but expressing emotions doesn't make us weak; it makes us human. Strength isn't just physical or mental toughness, nor is it about barricading yourself inside your feelings. Like anything under pressure, it eventually builds up.

We need healthier ways to communicate so it doesn't become a "moment" but rather a process for growth. You tell yourself you won't break down, but sometimes you do. It shatters you into pieces, and in silence, you're the one who has to pick them up. I think for men, especially those raised in the '70s, '80s, and '90s, this rings especially true. These things weren't discussed back then. It's time to change that narrative, breaking down the stigma and ego we cling to.

I made these changes because I wanted to be a better husband and a better father. I knew there were things I needed to work on to be fully present for my family. Alcohol and other "coping" methods only create temporary distractions, allowing you to avoid the real issues. They offer a momentary escape from the truth, but nothing more.

If I had to give advice on expectations, it would be this: No one is perfect. Strive to be happy, to be healthy, and to find your purpose in life that aligns with your values. That's the key. Once you've found that purpose, everything else supports your objective. Always remember that the person you are today isn't the person you'll be tomorrow. You're a work in progress, so give yourself permission to grow and experience life. I don't need to be 100% perfect; I just need an open mind and a resilient heart to learn and understand the lesson. As long as you're willing to put in the work, you're on the right path.

The other piece of advice is to not quit when things get hard. Embrace the challenge and be kind to yourself. Appreciate the journey, not just the destination. I was afraid to go through tough times because I didn't want to disappoint anyone, but I ended up with bitterness. I was afraid of messiness, afraid of change, and that led me to quit several times, nearly costing me everything. Now, it's personal.

When I say I quit, I don't mean just saying, "I'm done; I'm not doing this." I mean that I reached a point where I didn't want to live anymore. As a man of faith now, I see that as abandoning God and His love for me. I firmly believe He doesn't put you through adversity if He doesn't think you can handle it. There's always a lesson He wants you to learn through that process. It took me many years to understand this. I was fortunate that He built a community around me to guide me back to where I needed to be.

Even now, I continue working to understand it, because when life gets hard, we're tempted to ask, *Why me?* But we need to stop doing that. It's just life. There's a reason you're going through it; you just have to be patient to understand. Remember, if you don't work on this today, your time is short.

Time is finite. When we take our last breath and look back, we don't want to leave this world with regrets. Regret is a heavy burden that disrupts peace. If you've never experienced that moment of reflection, just remember: You may be young now, but someday you'll age. Work and live to be happy so that you can share that happiness with others. Tough moments in life aren't often appreciated at face value, but when you face similar challenges again, you'll at least have the tools to get through it based on your past experience.

Separate yourself from others' expectations, even if they come from good intentions. Define who you are and what you want to be. First, figure out what you want from life. Once you know that, you'll be in a better place to care for and love your loved ones without carrying the weight of expectations you placed on yourself. Take risks and bet on yourself; it's the greatest investment of your life. It's okay to grow and expand your limits because that's how you measure growth and evolution. Keep pushing those boundaries further, and you'll become a stronger person with each step.

Stop measuring your success by others' expectations or perceptions; instead, appreciate your journey to surpass your own limits.

As men, we need to stop thinking in terms of wins and losses. When you view life as wins and losses, you're focused solely on getting from point A to point B, overlooking the journey in between. But the journey is what matters most. Once we reach our goal, many of us think, *What now? Is this enough? I want more.* This makes it hard to appreciate the journey. Redefine success on your own terms because what might be a win for you may not be for others, and what you consider a loss might be different for someone else. Be kind to yourself.

The mistakes you make help shape who you are. Trying to be perfect is like walking a straight line—consistency is good, but there's no growth. With ups and downs, you know you've built resilience to get through tough moments, and that's what counts. You don't need anyone else's approval. Once you reach a place of self-understanding, no one else's approval will be as fulfilling as your own. Embrace the journey and the process because that's where true validation lies.

Be okay with being the underdog; it's a mindset. I've been an underdog my whole life, but being an underdog gives you an advantage because you're always looking up, ready to fight the uphill battle. When you reach the top, that's one more accomplishment to your credit. I learned that from my dad: Always prepare for all 12 rounds. It's preparation for your next battle.

There's a song I recently listened to that sums up this chapter perfectly. The quote that begins this chapter is from a song by Dax featuring Darius Rucker called "To Be a Man." I spent years living up to everyone else's expectations because I thought that was what I needed to do, but I was wrong. I take accountability for not speaking up for myself. Until I learned to do so, I created a path of self-destruction, and my vision was clouded. There's a powerful quote from the movie *Shawshank Redemption*: "Get busy living, or get busy dying." I just kept going. It doesn't get easier, but it gives you a perspective that brings meaning and impact. That's the expectation I live for now.

CHAPTER 2

"I will always do my duty no matter what the price.
I've counted up the cost. I know the sacrifice.
I don't want to die for you, but if dying is asked of me,
I'll bear that cross with honor."
–Toby Keith

This chapter is about sacrifice, a concept that means different things to different people. Often, when we think of sacrifice, we think of giving up something to make something else happen. I want to shift that perspective a bit. Here in this book, sacrifice means doing something different, breaking out of your comfort zone to serve a greater purpose, and knowing that the benefit of the action may not be in your favor. Yet, you continue to do it so that someone else may gain value out of it. Life and death balance each other on our journey, but most of us live cautiously, avoiding risks, while others step out of that "safe" position for a bit of risk to seek that deeper meaning. Sacrifice, when done wholeheartedly, is beautiful because it's no longer about you. It's about being fully present in a moment that calls on you to rise.

Sacrifice, to me, encompasses respect and love for others in a way that can deeply impact their lives. As a young man growing up in the '90s, I was selfishly defining myself, but the 2000s brought a time of national self-definition. My dad had always instilled in my brother and me that "being an American is a privilege, not a right." He sacrificed everything to cross the Pacific Ocean on a tiny "banana boat," facing countless dangers along the way. Being American, to him, was more than just holding a citizenship card or showing pride on holidays. It was an opportunity to build a future in "peace"—what we call the American Dream.

My dad immigrated to the United States in the late '70s, and I was born here in 1979. He attended community college and worked multiple jobs to take advantage of the opportunities available to him. My dad was a blue-collar worker, a skilled welder who was respected for his craft. He worked for a defense company, building the first Bradleys and Abram tanks used in Operation Desert Storm. Later, he worked for a major motor-cycle manufacturer. He was a proud man who put every ounce of energy into making sure his American-raised sons had every-thing they needed to succeed.

As an adult (depending on the day), a husband, and now a father, my dad's sacrifices mean even more to me as I reflect on everything he did for my brother and me. Looking back, there are a million things I was oblivious to growing up, but I always sensed that my dad's actions held deeper cultural meaning.

Sunday nights, we'd have family dinners—the one time each week we'd all gather after the week's preparations were done.

I remember one night, my brother and I were packing our lunches for a field trip using our prized lunchboxes. I had a *Dukes of Hazzard* one and a *Transformers* one that I took everywhere. (I wish I'd kept them—they'd be worth a lot now!) My dad, on the other hand, always brought his lunch in a simple paper bag with plastic containers. My brother and I would sometimes dig through his bag, hoping he'd brought home treats from work. One day, as we rummaged, we found an empty, faded Coke can in his lunch bag. I remember thinking we could recycle it to make some extra money toward a new Nintendo—a little side hustle for us in the '90s.

Curious, I asked, "Why do you keep that Coke can, Dad?" (Looking back, I'm surprised he answered. In our traditions, kids weren't expected to ask questions like that—it was usually, "Do as I say.") My dad explained, "It gets pretty hot at work with all the welding gear on, and a fresh cold soda would be great. But instead of buying a Coke every day, I fill up the can with water and pretend it's Coke." My brother and I were confused, so he went on, "The 35 cents I'd spend on a Coke each day adds up. Over a week, a month… that money can turn into something special, like a nice dinner out, or a trip to Chuck E. Cheese." At the time, this went right over my head—I didn't understand the sacrifice he was making. Instead of saying, "I love you," he showed us.

I didn't fully appreciate my dad's sacrifices until I became a father myself. Reflecting on how he raised me, I see now that he was a hard and tough man to please, but he was also a great man. Life handed him challenges, including starting over in a new "home" where he was a complete stranger, but my dad made sure my brother and I had the essentials we needed to survive. To clarify: he focused on what we *needed*, not what we *wanted*, because he didn't care about "extras" or the perceptions of "others." As long as we had a roof over our heads, food on the table, clothes to wear, and good grades, that was all that mattered.

My dad did all this for us—his legacy, his future—fulfilling choices he made long before we were even born. We were his purpose. He didn't care how uncomfortable or lonely he felt being away from his homeland and family. This was his "new dawn." And in the moment I first held my son, Clayton, I finally understood. I realized that my life was no longer just for me. I had my time, and now this was my decision. My life was for my family, for my son and daughter. This realization always brings a lump to my throat, and I tear up, finally understanding my dad's journey, which I had been blind to for so long. My dad has never accepted a "thank you" from us. He sees it as his duty and responsibility, even now, to be there for us and our families. Even at his age, he still feels responsible. He isn't building his American Dream; he's helping build ours, which has become his legacy.

In the 2000s, we as a country were rethinking what it meant to be American. September 11, 2001, changed all our lives in one way or another. The vulnerability we felt as a nation made me re-evaluate my own life. I had spent too many years coasting by, doing the bare minimum, so it was time for a change. My perspective had to mature because, for the first time, I was paying attention to a world that seemed unsettling. My brother enlisted in the Marine Corps shortly after 9/11 to change the course of his life, and while I was the "patriot" between us, I envied his commitment and courage.

At one point, I thought I wanted to be a police officer and was following that path, but that wasn't the plan God had for me. In 2005, due to California's political and financial struggles, budget cuts affected the state, including police departments.

That same year, I read an article that completely shifted my perspective. It described soldiers being deployed for extended periods beyond their 12 months, and how, when they returned, their young children didn't recognize them. This sparked a turning point for me. Every time I got close to the Chief's interview for a police officer position, something would go wrong. The economy and political climate in California hampered my plans. I was close, but never close enough, which made me consider the Army even more seriously. I wondered if I was considering it for the right reasons and mulled over it for several days.

It took a drunken Saturday night and a single question to sober me up fast. When God has plans for you, it doesn't matter what you want; He'll deliver what you need. My friends (at least ten of us) and I were sitting around a small Weber grill after a night out, using a Duraflame log as our fire pit. By early morning, we were deep in conversation. Then someone asked: *If you were to die today, what would people say about you?* As soon as the question was posed, I had a flashback "movie" moment, reflecting on my life, and I was not proud. I froze. Everyone else had something funny, sad, or happy to share, but I had nothing —not even a witty remark.

That moment couldn't have been clearer. I was 26 in February of 2006, and my purpose suddenly crystallized. I realized that I'd been living selfishly. I had somewhat put my life together, but I still couldn't figure out my next move. I had my own apartment, a job, and even a minivan to cruise around in (and yes...I thought I was cool, too), and yet I was discontent. There had to be more, I thought. Frustration set in. I had spent the last two years testing for police departments with no success. I had spent many years making mistakes I wasn't proud of, and my expectations of myself had changed.

The article, the question, and my faith all led me to this point. I was going to do something bigger than myself—an unselfish act to help others and to serve God's will. I wasn't trying to be a hero or a martyr. I just needed to fulfill God's purpose and bring true meaning to my life. I no longer wanted to feel lost; I wanted to go in a direction that would define me. I had often felt turmoil about what I needed to do, but this time was different. The Army would help me understand my limitations and push me to grow beyond them. I was determined, and though I was scared, it felt right. I didn't know what to expect, but that's where faith mattered. I was willing to give my life for this as long as I could help bring one soldier home to see their family. To me, that would make it all worth it.

I reported to the Army on March 23, 2006. It was time to grow up and become a man. This was my sacrifice, my contribution to being an American. For everything this country provided for my immigrant family, it was time to give back. Some may never see or accept me as an American because of my heritage, but I was born to bleed red, white, and blue. In this generation of the Tran family, I'm proud to say my dad has two American kids who were willing to fight for this country as a Marine and a Soldier. (I guess those lessons were never lost—I just needed to listen.)

I know I'm blessed. I didn't understand it as a kid, but as an adult, I realize how fortunate I am that my dad did all these things for me. Looking back through a different lens, I appreciate what I once saw as harsh or irrational conversations—times when I said, "Let me be me, Dad." He never let go of me; he kept holding on, providing me with more support and hope to keep going. He gave up on fully assimilating into American culture to preserve what he thought I needed to know about my heritage. Those long hours he worked, those endless conversations I once dismissed... I hear you now, Dad. I'm listening. You've done more for us than you have ever done for yourself, and I just want you to know how much I appreciate it. I'm sorry it took me so long to understand those moments. Thank you for being you and for sacrificing so much of your time for us.

My dad taught me a valuable lesson, and he is my true hero. When you make a sacrifice, you're not doing it to be a "hero;" you're doing what needs to be done, even if it's something most people aren't willing to do, without seeking recognition. Many heroes I have known are no longer with us. The word hero means different things to different people. Often, our ideas of heroes come from movies or comic books, but the principles are the same: They sacrifice for others and do it quietly, out of pure intention. These are the heroes who may never get to take another breath of freedom. I understand now that you earn that title when you give your all, and it's no longer about "you."

It really comes down to the question of "why." Why are we doing this, and who is it for? When you're doing something for attention, you're no longer doing it for the cause or for others; you're doing it for yourself. Just look at social media today—everyone seems to be seeking praise to boost their own agenda. (I'll call it that... and leave it at that.) I think it detracts from the impact you're trying to make. I had to ask myself the same question: *Did I understand who I was doing this for, and would I fulfill my purpose by helping a soldier get home to their family?* I needed to do

47

something beyond myself. I left my home to give another American a better chance at life, answering the call at a time when this country needed it most.

And I firmly believe in this. I am no hero. I'm just a man trying to do what I feel is the right "thing" for the betterment of this world and in service to God. I hope that one small, kind act leads to another in this vast universe.

One of the things I've come to appreciate about sacrifice is that it teaches you not to take anything for granted; you earn your peace and understanding, allowing you to rebuild yourself when given the chance. However, the perception of sacrifice is sometimes skewed by the desire for recognition. We live in a time where self-gratification is all over social media, just for the clicks. The act may be good, but the intentions are sometimes shallow. We all want to do good, but at times, we don't do what's necessary—we do what makes us look good in others' eyes. Where's the impact of that?

When I joined the Army, I was stripped of all entitlements the moment I arrived at 30th AG, Fort Benning, Georgia (now known as Fort Moore). I knew that when I said goodbye to my family and friends, they were saying goodbye to the old me, and I had to embrace this new foundation. This was going to be a transformation, not a sacrifice, because I chose to become a better version of myself. Time became meaningful, and I was tired of running in circles. No more excuses.

The Army made me earn everything back, even my last name (though for most of boot camp, my name was "Fatbody Roster number 147." I almost forgot my own name by the time I graduated (One Station Unit Training, otherwise known as OSUT!) I earned the "U.S. Army" patch, my uniform, my boots, and, most importantly, my blue Infantry cord. This process taught me to work hard, to appreciate the essentials, and to complete the mission with the minimum needed to survive. That's what being in the Infantry means to me. It's about relying on your brothers for success, whether you like them or not. I had been broken down and molded back together with pride. The sacrifice was the time I spent learning my limits and learning who I was. Sacrifice builds accountability; there is always room for improvement, but you have to give up something to gain something. Most importantly, through this process, I learned about myself. I understood my ceiling and what that potential meant and that there was more work to do.

I keep returning to the idea of impact because, in this lifetime if we don't create an honest impact, what are we doing? If we're not making changes that help others, what are we doing as a human race? Acts of kindness should mean setting aside ego for the greater good. The world is already divided by people's egos and their desire to be right or to be in the spotlight. One of our biggest downfalls as Americans is that we've stopped listening to each other. We don't want to sacrifice our opinions or consider others' perspectives because being "right" has become more important. The tug-of-war over who holds the position of power has overshadowed the simple act of taking a moment to understand another view. Investing a few minutes to bridge differences isn't a burden; it's an opportunity to grow.

As a veteran, I've had many conversations with people who think of the Infantry as "heartless monsters." My sacrifice in service to this country is beyond me, but I feel it's my duty to educate others, even those with opposing views, through my experience. These conversations are never easy, and sometimes I feel like a magnet for them, but people only know what they know until they listen. (I start off unconventionally by popping my eye out to get their attention… it works!) For example, people have told me that I went to war "for oil." Did I? Is there something they know that I don't?

When they ask what I did in the Army, I say I was in the Infantry, and they picture teams of "Rambos" running around, guns blazing, when in reality, we're so much more than that. It's sad to think that people view our sacrifices as acts of conquest when, in truth, our mission was to serve and protect those who couldn't protect themselves. The U.S. military does so much to rebuild and support communities on deployment, yet we're often misjudged based on a 20-second video clip.

When I put on my uniform, I didn't need anyone to know my name. I just needed people to know that I was fighting for freedom here and abroad. I've heard stories my whole life from my dad about how, in a single night, his freedom and way of life were taken away. His home and country were lost in a moment. I would never want to experience that, and I don't think the American people would either. That's the sacrifice of being an American. We have privileges that we need to protect because if we don't bridge our differences and truly listen, we risk losing it all to a stronger force. At that moment, we would be left with nothing.

True listening means understanding another person's perspective without needing to judge them as wrong or validate your own position. It's about being considerate—truly grasping how that person feels in that moment, at that time, and under-standing what's in their heart. That kind of listening makes sacrifice even more impactful. What we need more of is empa-thy, understanding, connection, and honest communication.

It's our duty to meet others halfway on that bridge: either to let them bring us to their side so we can build that connection or to take them to ours so they can understand. It's not about being right; it's about sharing perspectives. Don't be quick to say, "You're wrong." Be open to being wrong, too, so that you can grow and build.

When I signed those papers, I was ready to give my life to make the world a better place. I'm an idealist. Why can't we just have a conversation? Why can't we celebrate our differences in values and resolutions? That's where we stand apart, and I think it's a beautiful thing.

I know the balance will never be even. It will never be an equal path. Talking about sacrifice reminds me of a song by Toby Keith, "The American Soldier." I think of my guys— shout out to my Triple Deuce brothers (2nd Battalion 22nd Infantry, Anvil Company, circa 2006). These men helped me redefine who I am and my journey. Most importantly, they renewed my faith in humanity. They showed me what sacrifice is really about and helped me understand the intent and purpose behind our mission. No matter what others thought of us, we had an objective, and we were going to achieve it. The things we saw and endured will always be a part of us, and we gave a piece of ourselves to this country because we love it. The only way to heal is through conversation, faith, and each other.

Joining the Army was my sacrifice to this world. I'm not a martyr; I simply believe in something greater and knew I had to become more than I was before enlisting. I couldn't keep wandering through life without purpose. I came home with mental health issues, a titanium rod in my leg, broken arms and hands, and one eye. (I will discuss the event that caused this later in this book.) I am blessed to be alive, and it was all worth it. I wouldn't change a thing because of the lessons I gained.

People often ask if I regret it: there is no regret. When we made the decision, we knew what we were willing to leave behind.

In this lifetime, my combat brothers and I made sacrifices to better the lives of others, not just our own. Whatever comes next, I'll continue to look ahead and keep marching forward because this world is worth it, and you are worth it.

We are not heroes, just soldiers. "DEEDS NOT WORDS."

CHAPTER 3

"To live like you were dying, like tomorrow was a gift
and you've got eternity to think about
what you'd do with it."
–Tim McGraw

This chapter is about quitting, and quitting is like a cancer. Once it starts, it's hard to stop. I think most people do it every day. I did it for a long time, especially when it came to commitments, both to myself and to others, before joining the Army. Quitting is easy; it's always been the easy way out. Most people quit every day and still expect things to change. I was one of those people. But nothing changes when you quit; it only prolongs what you eventually need to face. Quitting echoes within you, slowly boxing in your potential. The only solution is to face it, be accountable, and learn from the setbacks to grow.

I believe that for 99 percent of people, quitting feels like the only option. But it takes that rare 1 percent to face adversity, to push through what needs to be resolved, and to come out the other side. We all go through phases in life when quitting feels acceptable, but there comes a time when you look in the mirror and realize it's too much to carry—doubts, insecurities, and fears start to weigh you down and ultimately lead to a lack of accountability. At that point, you're left asking yourself, *How do I go back and fix this?*

When you reach these critical thresholds, especially when you're younger, you need to know how to face them. Make each challenge a mental exercise to overcome, building resilience into your mindset. Embrace the struggle, change your perception of obstacles, and recognize that the hard road is often the best one. You don't always have to hit the "home run" or "grand slam." Those who do it consistently are rare, but you're unique in your own way. You don't have to do it alone, but you have to want it for yourself. People can't carry you forever. That's the lesson I had to learn.

In high school, everything was easy for me. I had a 3.7 GPA and kept it on "cruise control," even while trying to act like a "hood" kid. As I mentioned before, I'd hang out with my crew, but as soon as the lights came on, I'd run back home like a good little puppy. But it was easy because I had people who held me accountable—mainly my dad. My dad and I had a 7 p.m. check-in every day on the clock when he'd call on his lunch break. I'd always have to tell him exactly what I was doing, and he would give me guidance. However, when I left for college in my freshman year at UCSB, that accountability was gone. I was immature and didn't know how to be responsible for myself. To be real, I was arrogant and reckless. I thought I "knew it all," and my ego was through the roof. I saw myself as tough and gritty, but I was really lacking action and determination.

That freshman year in college showed me I wasn't ready for anything—I was a quitter. Some people may be shocked to hear that, but there's no way around it. I have to be accountable now. At some point, you must confront the reality that something has to change, and part of that change is facing why you didn't fight through it. Otherwise, the problem will always be you. You can't keep complaining and blaming others. Remember, when you point fingers at someone else for your failures, three fingers are pointing back at you.

The real issue was that I got a taste of freedom and thought I no longer needed to put in the work. I figured it would be easy, like high school—that I could just rely on my intelligence and coast through. The result? I landed on academic probation in the first and second quarters and was disqualified by the end of my freshman year. I blamed everyone else—the professors, my classmates, anyone I could think of: "The professor sucked" or "They just didn't like me." But how could they like me or do their job well if I never even showed up to class? It was like living *Ferris Bueller's Day Off* for a whole year. Sure, I got into great physical shape, and maybe my basketball game improved (it didn't), but I chose "being cool" over doing what I needed to do.

I never put in the work. I'd throw something together two hours before class, right before an assignment was due, and this became a bad habit. The consequence was that I was terrified to tell my dad I'd been kicked out because of the high expectations he had set for me. I had defied those expectations, and I blamed my dad for not setting them for myself. In that thought alone, the "cancer" of quitting truly took root.

I knew I had messed up, and then I fell into self-pity, making it feel okay to just move on to something else. I didn't finish anything. I felt the weight of letting my family down, and the worst part was that I lied to my dad—and, most importantly, to myself. I had no balance, no real boundaries. I limited myself, gave up when things got hard, and boxed myself into failure. The simple solution was to reset, start over, and put in the work. I could give you every excuse in the world, but none of them would matter enough to validate how I felt. I felt like a loser. Correction: I *was* a loser. I wanted the freedom of adulthood and to manage my own life, but I wasn't ready for it.

I was free to see the world, and I saw parts of it that I probably wasn't mature enough to handle. Alcohol was involved, and smoking a lot of marijuana became a coping mechanism to numb the guilt and thoughts in my head. My friends used it recreationally; I was using it to escape. I got myself into trouble and couldn't handle the pressure. At one point, I even ended up detained for things I shouldn't have had on me. I was lucky to walk away with only volunteer work as a consequence. Looking back, I'm not proud of that moment. But I've grown, and my life now is night and day from what it was then. What was I thinking? Truth is, I wasn't. I was only thinking of myself. It was easier to walk away than to deal with the problems I'd created. Accountability was a real issue, even in my relationships and friendships. I even thought of escaping this world. I didn't know how to deal with my own feelings; I was like a zombie with no intentions or purpose. Nothing changed because I didn't want to change.

I went to the gym with my buddy every day, but when it came to class, I might show up once a week, if that. I was extremely fit but mentally weak. So weak that I almost took my own life off the sixth floor of my dorm room because I couldn't face the reality of my poor decisions. Angels are among us, and mine was Silas Pompa, my resident assistant, who stepped in when I needed him most. (I thank you, Silas, for being there, a big brother to the end. Silas passed a few years ago from cancer, and he will always be honored in my life. This is how I honor you, brother—with my truth.)

How did it get so bad that I was on the edge of my life, thinking that was the best option? I was blessed to have Silas there, providing the support I needed at that moment. I had no idea what I was doing. I took the screen off the window, sitting there in tears. Not because of bad grades—I was in tears because I felt sorry for myself and kept asking, *Why? How did I let this happen? How did I let things go this far? Why was I such an idiot?* I sat there, teetering between life and death because I couldn't face the truth. But Silas gave me hope and, more importantly, grace. He said, "You're being way too hard on yourself. These are just grades. This isn't what really matters in life. What matters is how you get back up and face this moment. It's never too late until God says it's your time." (An ironic statement that would later have an even deeper impact on my life.) "This is a defining moment. You'll figure it out, one piece at a time, to change yourself and your situation." I knew he was right. I took his hand and returned back inside with anguish but also with a seed of determination to course-correct and hope to make it out okay.

At some point, I had to tell my dad that I failed (though I never told him about my attempt). My friends would eventually know I was a quitter, or maybe they already knew and just hadn't said anything. It wasn't their responsibility. This was the consequence of my poor decision-making. I remember my dad crying and pleading with me to come home… but I knew I couldn't. The whole "My house, my rules" thing was too much. I'd tasted freedom, and I didn't want to go back. It broke me to know that I'd hurt him and, even more so, that I'd shattered the image of the son he thought I'd become. He was disappointed. He never expressed it, but there was that one look: the look of shattered expectations, all the hard sweat and tears he'd invested in me. At that moment, I felt like I'd broken his "American Dream."

I knew I had messed up, and I had to muster every bit of willpower I had left to dig myself out of this hole. The reality was this: I had been a 3.7 GPA student in high school, but now I had a 0.16 GPA in my first quarter of college, and by the end of the year, I was barely above a 1.17. How was I going to climb my way out? Even a miracle wouldn't fix this. The only way forward was to start over from the beginning and get to work on the mess I'd created. I'd lost my full-ride scholarship to UCSB. I was working two jobs while retaking classes at Santa Barbara Community College. One day at a time, for a year, I juggled two to three jobs during what should have been my sophomore year to earn my way back to UCSB on academic probation.

I owe a lot to that school and to the faculty at the Equal Opportunity Program (EOP), who never gave up on me. Mr. Ozzie and Miss Lupe were my unsung heroes, helping me find my way back to campus. Unfortunately, by the time I returned to UCSB, life had taken me in another direction, and I was called home for a personal family matter that I choose not to share here. My chance at UCSB was over. My time at that beautiful Southern California coastal school, my "home away from home," was a memory of an immature young boy facing hard lessons. But I did find parts of myself there—friends who became family, a big brother who saved my life, "puppy love," and unforgettable moments. Still, the experience was tainted by the way I'd given up on myself and my responsibilities. Life was calling, and it was time to answer.

My expectations were unrealistic and unattainable. They were skewed from reality and shallow in vision. I had chosen not to see the truth. Looking back, if I could talk to that 20-year-old version of myself… forget that, I'd give him a swift kick in the ass to jumpstart his life! Most importantly, I'd tell him to be honest and accountable. Quitting is an evolution that leads you straight into denial. No one wants to admit it, and we tend to blame others. It's even harder when others recognize it in you. At some point, though, quitting brings you to a crossroads.

You can keep running, but quitting just keeps you running in place. You're not going anywhere, and it costs you time. Time is the one thing we can't change or recover. You only get this one opportunity in each moment, and then life moves on. The path ahead is determined by each decision, one after another. I was lost, but I almost lost it all.

As I slowly regained my confidence in the years following that college disaster, my next valuable lesson came to me in the Army. I'd been in my unit for a few months. Anvil Company had just returned from deployment, which I'd heard was brutal, and half of the 1st Platoon's senior leadership was concluding their service. With gaps in the squad lineup, I was promoted to team leader for the Weapons Squad. This promotion inflated my ego, creating a false sense of confidence. At 26, I was one of the oldest soldiers in my platoon, yet many of my peers, despite being younger, had far more combat experience. I worked hard to earn their respect, but until I had deployed and earned a combat patch on my shoulder, I knew I would never fully be seen as one of them.

There's a clear distinction between those who have seen combat and those who haven't. Some leaders understood this divide, and some didn't. Earning respect is a tradition, a rite of passage for new soldiers in a unit—especially for "cherries," as the newest soldiers are called. I hated being a cherry, especially as a team leader, because it put me in an uncomfortable spotlight. The "E4 Mafia" was brutal. I was also a target because I was a "college E4"—I hadn't earned the rank through merit or time but was given it for having a college degree. I agreed 100 percent: I didn't feel I deserved it either. When I enlisted, I had already avoided the conversation about Officer Candidate School (OCS) because I knew I wasn't prepared to lead a group of men without combat experience. It didn't feel right to me, so I chose the enlisted route instead. And here I was, caught in a "damned if you do, damned if you don't" scenario. I tried not to let it get to me, but the truth is, I let it get the best of me—and I failed.

One morning, the assignment was to put on a 25-pound pack (rucksack) and complete a five-mile road march. I did what I was supposed to do—I grabbed a rice bag from my closet to make weight (yes, I'm that person; that's a story for another time). A lot of the guys didn't meet the weight requirement, and I knew it. I was one of the few who actually complied, while others had stuffed their bags to appear full, marching with lighter loads. It gave me an attitude, and I was more focused on their b*llsh*t than on myself. That day, we also had some leadership changes, with our squad leader absent. Another sergeant (Sgt. A. Deciccio) took over, which annoyed me—I wondered why I wasn't leading the squad. Now, looking back, I know why: I wasn't ready. I had taken the title and rank and made myself feel important for superficial reasons—I wanted to feel like I mattered.

We started the road march, packs on, heading down the River Ridge Loop. At the halfway point, we turned to head back up a steep hill. I was already in a sour mood, and as Sgt. Deciccio shouted for us to move faster and finish strong, my bitterness grew. I was resentful, thinking about how I had carried the full weight while others hadn't, and I was at the back of the formation, falling behind. I'm 5'4" and a half (yes, I count my half-inch—because it matters to me). My stride was shorter than the others', and it felt like I was being left in the dust. Exhausted and frustrated, I cracked halfway up the hill. I didn't have the willpower to power through… and I stopped. I told Sgt. Deciccio that I was done and started throwing my squad under the bus, pointing out that others hadn't carried the same weight. Yes, in that moment, I became a blue falcon—a "buddy f*cker."

At that moment, I knew I'd messed up. Sgt. Deciccio was in the middle of pushing us up the hill when I said what I said. His eyes squinted, and he shot me a look that told me he was done. He got right in my face, screaming about how I'd let my guys down and urging me to finish. Stubborn, I refused, saying, "I'm not f*cking doing this anymore. You didn't check anyone else's bag; at least I'm carrying the correct weight." I was an idiot. He went red in seconds, his eyes practically bulging. I'm surprised he didn't take a swing at me because I probably would have if I'd been in his shoes. I tried to justify myself, missing the entire lesson because I was focused only on myself. No wonder I wasn't chosen to lead; I was self-righteous, and I had just quit right in front of my team. Every ounce of respect I'd earned was lost in that moment. He gave me every chance to make it right before I threw my bag down.

He said, "Tran, pick it up and finish it out."

I looked at him and said, "No. I'm the one carrying the right amount of weight, and yet you're yelling at me instead of anyone else."

His response? "I'm gonna ask you one more time, Tran. Are you going to continue this road march? Are you going to quit?"

I replied, "You know what, f*ck it. I'm going to quit."

Then he gave me a courtesy warning in a low voice: "Let me give you a fair warning: if you quit on your guys on the battlefield, someone will pay the price because you were too weak to carry on."

I just stared at him. I made a weak excuse that my knees were hurting.

He picked up my bag and handed it to my buddy, who was also a team leader at the time, Spc. A. Oliver and told me to watch as my team carried my burden. "You're being a little bitch. You're going to let him suffer the next two and a half miles so you can watch him carry your weight."

I never forgot that moment. As you can see, it's been 16 years since my medical retirement from the Army, and I still remember it as if it happened just the other day. I didn't want to quit, but I did. I f*cked up... like really f*cked up. I did it because I was selfish. My ego and pride were much more important at that moment. I thought of only myself and not my team. At that moment, I did not acknowledge it, but reflecting afterward... I did.

We made it back to the battalion, and Sgt. Deciccio didn't say another word to me. I apologized to my team and squad as soon as we returned, but it was an empty apology—the damage to my credibility was already done. There was only one person responsible for that moment: me.

A couple of days went by, and Sgt. Deciccio pulled me aside to check on me and to explain why that moment had mattered so much to him. On the deployment they'd just returned from, they had lost a few soldiers—brothers. He needed me to understand that his reaction wasn't personal, yet in some ways, it was.

It was personal for me, too. It was a moment for growth, but my ego was bruised. Sgt. Deciccio had hit my pride, and rightfully so. I needed to be reminded that this wasn't about me—it was about the soldiers depending on me for guidance. I failed miserably at that moment, but I swore to myself it would be the last time. Enough was enough. I hadn't just quit on myself; I quit on my team. Most importantly, I quit on him, and in doing so, I created a stigma around myself, one that I wasn't ready or good enough. I had no one to blame but myself, but for the longest time, I held a grudge against Sgt. Deciccio. I couldn't stand hearing his name, and I couldn't stand looking at him. I was determined to prove him wrong. I know now it wasn't right, but that determination eventually became a pivotal moment of clarity—a lesson that wouldn't come until years later and would help me recover.

I eventually earned back my squad's trust. My brothers knew I was more than that one moment and that I wouldn't betray their trust again. I was very grateful for that—a second chance. I understood that wearing the uniform was a privilege and that the mission was always going to be bigger than me.

I didn't learn to appreciate Sgt. Deciccio until I was severely injured on Mother's Day in 2008. It was one of the most painful and disorienting moments of my life. I didn't recognize who I was, and once again, I was at a crossroads. Each day of recovery,

I faced myself in the mirror, trying to piece myself back together. I'd lost my right eye, had a titanium rod placed in my left leg, and had shrapnel embedded all over my face. I couldn't fathom why I was still alive. Tears and doubt ran down my face daily—I hid my pain from people so I wouldn't burden them.

I was struggling, and every day, I asked myself, *Is this the day you're going to quit? Because if you don't accept yourself, how can you expect anyone else to accept you?* I'd told my friends before I deployed that I knew I wouldn't come back the same, but this was not what I'd meant. I felt like I was dying inside, watching my family and friends endure the beginning of my recovery—especially my dad. It was unbearable, and I didn't feel worthy of their love.

Then I heard his voice again in my mind—un... f*cken... believable: *"Are you going to quit again, Tran?"* Of all people, it was Sgt. Deciccio's voice. What the hell! I could hear him yelling at me, saying that if I quit again, someone would get hurt. In the end, the one who got hurt was me. I was angry... actually, I was angry for a long time. I was trying to make sense of why I was still alive. *God, why did you keep me alive? What's my purpose now? I failed again... I did not complete my mission.* And I hadn't done anything wrong the night I got blown up.

But then I decided, *No, I'm not going to do it. I'm not going to let anyone—especially him—yell at me for quitting.* Because if I quit again, I'd never hear the end of it. People would say I was never a fighter. I had fought against all odds up to this point, and this was just another moment I needed to get through. I was exhausted and hurting, but I needed to trust that there was a reason I was still here.

I understood what I'd signed up for, but I guess I hadn't really thought about what it would mean to be injured. My view was simple: live or die—but I never considered the gray area of being wounded. I knew I couldn't put my dad through more pain, and proving Sgt. Deciccio wrong became my motivation. I realize now that I wasn't always thinking rationally. But I had to do what was needed to get out of that hospital. I hated Walter Reed—it was time to break free from that prison.

But it was his voice and message that helped carry me through those hard times. Years later—probably around 2013— we lost one of our brothers. It was a time when many of us who survived the war found it harder to cope with life back home. For some, the pressure and changes were too overwhelming, and thoughts of not being present in this world seemed like an easier escape. I've been there, and while I don't judge their actions, I understand now that we, the survivors, are left holding pieces of a puzzle that we can no longer piece together. Death has a way of bringing the living back together, yet pain often divides us from those we've lost.

I heard that Sgt. Deciccio was checking up on the guys who'd heard the news of our brother's demise. Many of them planned to attend the funeral, but I couldn't make it. However, I knew I needed to reach out to Sgt. Deciccio and make things right. I needed to apologize for my actions, take accountability, and let him know I finally understood the lesson he'd taught me. Without realizing it, he'd given me the strength to get through the biggest test of my life. I endured 15 months and came out stronger. When I finally tracked him down and called, I said, "Hey Sgt., it's Tran." He was thrilled to hear from me, mentioning that he'd heard what had happened but didn't have my information to check in.

I reminded him of our moment, and he chuckled, recalling it

right away. He said, "I don't remember if we ever talked after that."

"Oh, we did," I replied. "You called me a 'little b*tch.'"

We both laughed, and he said, "Some time has passed, Tran. I'm really sorry about that. I was dealing with things myself, and you happened to hit a nerve at that moment."

I said, "Please don't apologize. That lesson saved my life during a long period of darkness." He asked what I meant, and I explained, "After I was injured, every time I felt like quitting, I heard your voice yelling at me not to quit."

He laughed hard, saying, "Was I really that bad?"

I told him, "No, it was exactly what I needed. I needed to face myself, battle my demons, and stop flying under the radar."

He said, "Same here, Tran. You're not alone."

I thanked him for not giving up on me and for teaching me such a valuable life lesson. I admitted, "Every time I heard your name, I'd get mad, but now I'm just grateful I had the chance to thank you."

His final words to me were, "I'm proud of you, Tran, you stubborn, grudgeful motherf*cker!" We laughed because it was true: I'd held onto that grudge to push through rehab.

I share this story because it was a powerful moment of accountability and understanding. Sgt. Deciccio and I shared a mutual respect as combat brothers, and I'm honored to have had the chance to express my gratitude to him. Sadly, that was the last conversation we had. I tell this story to honor him. He taught me resilience and mental strength. "Until Valhalla, brother—we'll meet again."

If you're reading this book and you're someone who struggles with adversity or wants to run when things get hard, fight to stay in it. It's not about winning or losing; it's about the journey. Wins and losses are just results, but the real lessons and growth come in between. Take responsibility for your actions—or lack of action. Recognizing and owning up to your actions is the first step. Then, looking in the mirror and accepting the person you see is another battle. It's an evolution and a work in progress. Stop making excuses and start taking charge of your life. It won't always look "pretty," and that's okay.

The moment I was injured gave me a different perspective on life. I've been blessed with a second chance—something many people who deserve it never get. I have to trust in my faith and God's reason for keeping me here. Quitting is not an option because I still have a purpose to find and fulfill.

It's always about progress. Life is a 12-round fight. Stop looking down on yourself, and take it one round at a time. The fleeting satisfaction of quitting lasts for a moment, but shortcuts never lead where you need to go. It's about facing trials, embracing the struggle, and rising above your challenges to see the vision of where you're meant to be.

Change the perception. The journey is really where you build your character. The song "Live Like You Were Dying" by Tim McGraw captures the spirit of this. I recommend you listen to it. Also, consider these questions: What can you do to improve yourself for tomorrow? Are you willing to fight yourself? Are you willing to be the greater version of yourself every day? As an excellent saying recommends, "Stop being great for the world, just be great for yourself."

CHAPTER 4

"Wake me up when September ends, falling from the stars,
drenched in my pain again, becoming who we are
as my memories rest, but never forget what I lost."
–Green Day

I believe we can all agree that losing someone is never easy. It's a difficult process, and there's no "right" amount of time to heal. Everyone's healing journey is different, shaped by their perception of loss and faith. I really dislike the saying, "Time will heal itself." It's only partially true because the other half of the equation is about what you do with the time to heal.

At some point, you can only hope life settles back into a "new normal" without that person there. But the truth is, it never does. A part of you is missing, leaving a void that nothing quite fills. One of the hardest aspects of loss is the thought, "I should have done more." That feeling of not doing enough brings a certain regret, which is often the most difficult part to handle. Regret can be overwhelming, undermining your thoughts and actions and leaving your mind constantly replaying the "what could I have done" or "what should I have done" scenarios. It becomes a quiet, persistent presence—a benign cancer that you can't seem to get rid of. Over time, this guilt can creep in and make you feel unable to move on, trapping you in your own "phantom zone," as depicted in the series *Smallville*. (I am a nerd… and proud of it.)

Life doesn't stop for you to figure it all out; it keeps moving forward. For me, I blinked, and suddenly, I'd been carrying this loss for 13 years. This particular loss was profound, shaking my principles, faith, and sense of purpose. The guilt of being alive consumed me for years, especially because it felt so beyond my control. I questioned why some people were given more time on this earth while good people seemed to leave before their time. I questioned God; my faith was fragile. None of it made sense.

On February 5th, 2008, we lost Sgt. Timothy Van Orman in Iraq. I remember it like it was yesterday. No one should ever have to experience a twenty-one-gun salute for a fellow soldier during deployment or stand and render a final salute to a brother-in-arms—but it happens.

Sgt. Van Orman's death was more than a loss; for me, it was a personal failure. It struck at the core of my beliefs. I've mentioned that I was an idealist—maybe I still am. Sgt. Van Orman was part of my purpose. I didn't join the Army to be a hero or a martyr; I just wanted to do something bigger than myself, to give my life meaning. For 13 years after Sgt. Van Orman's passing, I felt that he should be here living his life while I took his place. I felt undeserving of the chance to be here, living my life in this moment, while he misses everything today and beyond. Part of the reason I joined the Army was to give another soldier the chance to go home to see their family. I bottled up that feeling, and sometimes it would spill out, difficult to contain. In the veteran community, we often call this our "demon" because guilt can become a haunting, destructive force. Guilt kills your spirit and life.

Sgt. Van Orman and I had a mutual respect. We weren't best friends, but we were friends, and I respected him. I looked forward to our conversations when we crossed paths in the barracks hallway, especially when he was in charge of quarters (CQ). I often saw him at the CQ desk, and sometimes his wife, Cadie, would come by to drop off his dinner. I remember when we got our deployment orders and hearing that his wife was pregnant.

Sgt. Van Orman was a humorous, intelligent person with a bit of a quirky side. We initially connected over a conversation about college courses. It was one of those rare moments when the "college E4" label worked in my favor as I told him how I'd barely graduated with a 2.0 GPA. Everyone in the barracks assumed, because I was Asian and older, that I was smart—little did they know I was far from it (LOL). One of my favorite memories was watching him one weekend skinning some part of a deer and thinking how wild it was to do that right out in the open. (I was a California suburbia kid who, before the Army, had never known anyone who hunted.)

Sgt. Van Orman is a hero in my book. He was an outstanding soldier and leader, and I often saw him taking care of his team in the 2nd Platoon. He was also a good man, excited about becoming a father. Coping with his loss was one of the hardest challenges of my life. It took me a long time to redefine and understand my faith as I worked through the anger, sadness, and desperation for his death to somehow make sense. He'd volunteered for a mission that wasn't his, eager to contribute, and I remember our last interactions the evening before he left. Military humor isn't for everyone, but it finds a way into even heavy moments. I had just come out of the shower, as only a select few were heading out that night on a mission. As I walked out, I saw Sgt. Van Orman in passing. He always had something to say, so he joked, "You smell good. You getting ready for me tonight?" I laughed and told him to get in line and wait his turn, and he responded with one of his signature looks, raising his eyebrows in that familiar, playful way.

We chatted about his family, and he was beaming about his daughter, who had been born just before we deployed. He was a proud dad and loved to share updates and pictures of how she was doing. He invited me to come over later and see how big she'd gotten. I told him I'd be there when he got back from this mission. A few hours later, I saw him again in the chow hall, shoveling food as if he hadn't eaten in days. We teased him, telling him to slow down and that no one was going to steal his food. His response sticks with me: "Come on, boys, I'm hungry —and what if this is my last meal? I've got to eat as much as I can." We told him to shut up because it felt almost taboo to say something like that before heading out on a mission.

When the helicopters (the "birds") arrived, it was time for him to go. Sgt. Van Orman and a small group from our company, along with soldiers from the 82nd Airborne, prepared to leave. Hours passed, and we waited anxiously for updates. Then, we received a message back at the compound—it wasn't good. Anger spread through Anvil Company like wildfire. We were devastated, furious, and ready to take action. Some of us asked if we were going to suit up and roll out, but leadership told us to hold back as they gathered more intel. We wanted to go hunting; these were our brothers. Several were wounded, and some had been killed in action, but we didn't know who until confirmation came through. Each one of us in Anvil Company felt as if our souls had been torn from our bodies, filled with rage and grief. We were ready to unleash, but we had no orders to move, only to console each other and stand by.

I remember questioning God, asking, "Why didn't you take me?" That was why I was here, right? My objective and purpose seemed to slip from my grasp yet again. My personal mission was incomplete. Forget about my own injuries—standing in formation for the 21-gun salute in Iraq to say goodbye to a soldier, friend, and remarkable human being was the hardest thing I've ever had to do. Sgt. Van Orman deserved more time to be a husband and father. For over a decade, I've carried the weight of that day—the agony, guilt, and deep sense of loss. People say, "Trust the process," but that's hard to accept when it feels so unjust. I didn't know who to blame, and I still question God at times. And yet, I'm the one alive to feel this while he can't. I can only imagine what my brothers in the 2nd Platoon feel. Sgt. Van Orman and I were friends, but he was more than that—he was my combat brother, and that bond weighs heavily, especially because he embodied my ideal of service.

His death wasn't the only loss I suffered during deployment. I also lost my grandmother, and with her, I broke a promise that I could never fulfill. Earlier in this book, I mentioned that my father left his country and family to start a new life after the war. The family I knew in the States consisted of uncles and aunts who left for the same reason. I never knew my grandparents or extended family back in Vietnam. The Tran family was prestigious before the Tet Offensive; my father told my brother and me that if the war hadn't broken out, we'd have grown up like little princes in Vietnam. Our family held a position of prominence in the military due in part to my grand-uncle, Admiral Van Chon, whom I had the honor of calling Grandfather. He was the closest thing to a grandparent I had.

In 1996, when the borders opened for Vietnamese refugees who had not been back since they left, my dad and our family were finally able to visit Vietnam. We traveled as a family, and it was the first time I met my grandmother, my dad's mom. We bonded instantly. She was gentle, kind, and had a sense of humor, just like my dad. My Ba Noi (grandmother in Vietnamese) showed her love by spoiling me with food and quietly watching my brother and me with a smile. She used to giggle, calling me cute because I was round and chubby. (I would say "pudgy," but that's just me!) As a kid, I remember asking my mom why I didn't have grandparents here in the U.S. like my friends did—a loaded question for both my parents. I felt alone on Grandparents' Day at school, watching other kids' grandparents visit while I sat feeling left out.

This trip meant everything to me. It was short, but the wait to meet my Ba Noi had felt like an eternity. I was just grateful for the chance to hug her—many times. I promised her I'd come back to visit, but she passed away in April 2008, just two weeks before I was injured on Mother's Day during my deployment. I had a hard time saying goodbye when we left Vietnam, but it was even harder to know I'd never get one last hug. My dad was with her when she passed, and he told me that she had asked about me in her last days. I still carry her picture in my wallet because she's also one of my angels. I'm grateful to have had even a short time with her rather than never knowing her at all.

They say bad things come in threes, and during this deployment—and afterward—it felt that way.

After the deployment, it just seemed like we couldn't stop losing people. Many of the brothers I served with transitioned back home, and while people assume we're safe at home, the real battle often starts when the sounds of war go silent. We're left with thoughts and emotions that can't be shared with just anyone; only our band of brothers, who face their own battles, truly understand. It's not for lack of trying on anyone's part—it's just that anyone who wasn't there can never fully understand. So, we suffer in silence, trying not to burden anyone else, including our brothers. But when the "voice" inside gets too loud, there's no peace.

We become so accustomed to chaos that the calm feels unnatural, as if we're standing still while the world moves on. For about five or six years, some of us would get late-night calls. We knew what it meant. The pranks and drunken calls had stopped—now, they were somber calls with news of another loss. Over time, you become numb to it. That's the dangerous part of loss: when the pain no longer stirs you, and it just becomes another call. Life itself seems to lose its value when loss becomes a "part of life."

Society and the media call this PTSD. But I get so damn angry at that label because it oversimplifies what we go through. They call it a "transition problem" with symptoms and diagnoses, but they'll never fully understand. We don't trust people to understand where we're coming from or our feelings because, ultimately, they label and categorize us. Our losses have become a stigma in society. Don't sympathize with us—empathize. We don't need fixing; we just need a safe space to release the anguish when we're ready so we can begin to heal.

Loss is an evolution of emotions that can't be processed instantly because, in those moments, we're too numb to feel anything. Then comes anger, and eventually, numbness over-takes the feelings entirely. You lose that drive for self-preserva-tion and start questioning everything—your faith, your life. *Why am I still here? Why do I get to be with my family? What would they be doing if they were still here?* The weight of guilt follows, though, in reality, we're blessed to have this chance. But it's hard to let go. We worry that moving on means leaving them behind, yet we're the ones left behind if we don't let life move forward.

That was my journey for a very long time. I never spoke of it, but the thoughts ran through my head constantly. I would smile as if everything was okay, but inside, there was this bittersweet feeling—I was here, and he was not. I tried to honor him as best as I could, checking in with his wife to see how their family was doing. It felt like something I needed to do. One request from his wife was for me to write a letter to his daughter so she could learn about Sgt. Van Orman. What was supposed to be a simple request ended up taking me nearly 13 years to fulfill. *How do I write this letter?* I wondered. *What do I say to his daughter?* "Hey, young lady… I failed my mission in life… and he's no longer here… I'm sorry…" I was so angry at God: "Lord, why is it always the good people who have to leave us so soon?"

I didn't know how to put it into words. I prayed and prayed, hoping to find the right words for his daughter, but I kept hesi-tating. Part of me knew that writing this letter meant closing a chapter in my life—a moment that had made me grow up and become a man. I was grateful for how it had matured my perspective, but I was also sad, feeling like I would be letting go of a part of myself. I would look at my beautiful family and feel a gripe of sorrow, knowing he couldn't experience the joy that I was feeling at those moments. So much time had passed. I kept those feelings to myself, but it was exhausting. I would just smile for the world and "carry on."

This pain and anger kept me alive, kept me fighting through life without quitting—for me and for him. I was afraid that if I let this go, I wouldn't know who I was without it or if I'd have the strength to endure. I don't know the answer to that. The hurt of his loss felt so much greater than my own injury if I'm being honest. But I knew I had to honor him for his daughter; she was growing up and needed to know the great man and soldier he was.

During this process, I sought help and put in the work to finally express that pain so that I could heal and improve my mental health. I teared up, then cried as I wrote this letter, knowing that this was my goodbye. It was time for me to move on, not to forget him, but to finally fill the void and make myself whole again. Below is the letter I wrote to his strong, amazing, resilient daughter:

May 7, 2020

Dear Miss Halie,

This letter is long overdue to you. I have contemplated for 12 years how to write it. Your mom asked me to do this a long time ago, and I promised her that I would. But this was going to be the toughest task I had ever done. My biggest fear in writing this letter is that it would make you feel sad or at a loss again, but I agree with your mom that you need to know how great of a man your father was in this world and what he meant to me and your other uncles in the Triple Deuce (2nd Battalion 22nd Infantry Regiment Anvil Company).

For you to understand why your dad, Sgt. Timothy Van Orman, meant a lot to me, I am going to have to explain to you why I joined the Army. You see, back in 2006, I was a young man who lived a very selfish life. I had just recently graduated from college two years prior, had my own apartment, a good job and didn't have to really think about anybody else except for myself. I was 26 years old at the time, but I knew something was missing from my life. Service.

I am a man of faith, as people say… Fate would play its role when I picked up a Time *magazine and in the article it stated that soldiers were being deployed beyond their 12 months to even almost 20 months away from their families. What got me the most in that article was that they were saying that a lot of families who had soldiers deployed, some of their kids didn't even know who their mommies and daddies were, when they were finally able to come home, or some of them just didn't make it back home. I spent hours and days thinking about it, and I couldn't shake that thought off.*

You can call me an idealist (ask Mom what that means), but within a week or so, I enlisted in the Army in March of 2006. Of all the jobs I could have picked, I chose the Infantry. I felt that if I enlisted, I would be able to relieve one soldier from the front line to come home and be with their children along with their loved ones. I honestly and truly believed that. This was going to be my purpose… my main mission in the Army.

As fate would have it again, this is where Sgt. Van Orman and I would cross paths. Your dad was my principal. I truly believed that I was going to be able to make a difference.

*I want to be clear that your dad and I were not best friends, but we knew each other in Anvil Company. I was in 1st Plt. and he was in 2nd Plt. but we crossed paths every day. Your dad was a **good leader**, and **people respected him**. You can always tell when he talked, the soldiers would listen and that was always a strong sign of respect. Even in my platoon, they would acknowledge him with love and respect... and that normally does not happen because we are so competitive with each other.*

*As a new soldier to the company, your dad treated me differ-ently. He gave me a lot of respect when I was still trying to earn my place in the company. He knew that I was a college graduate, and we talked about school when he was at the CQ desk (ask Mom). This is how we originally connected through our passing through the halls. Eventually, when I would see him there and check to see how school was going or whatever he was cutting up after his hunting sessions (small talk, ya know). Every now and then, I would see your mom there visiting him when he was on CQ duty, and I do remember him sharing with me on how excited he was that he was going to be a father. Sgt. Van Orman's smile was like from ear to ear when-ever he talked about the family or you. This is one of my favorite memories of your dad; just **pure happiness**... it always made me feel that was such a great example in my life to be like that whenever I was supposed to have a family of my own. I can tell you this for sure: some of your other uncles in the Triple Deuce did not have the same feelings towards their* *family so his compassion and love for you and your mom was golden for me.*

I could feel his sadness one night before we were deploying in September of 2007. I know leaving you and your mom on his second deployment was not easy for him. I could sense his worry: sometimes you don't have to say it, but it was written on his face. Just like every good leader, Sgt. Van Orman pressed on because duty was calling. That's what we do as soldiers: we sacrifice what we love to defend others.

*During certain times on our deployment, I would cross paths with your dad and check on him on how you and your mom were doing (1st Plt. and 2nd Plt. were not always together doing the same thing). He would always shine his smile and offered to show me pictures whenever I was in the area. **Sgt. Timothy Van Orman loved you Halie**… he was always so excited when I asked him in passing.*

*Sadly enough, that last conversation that I had with him was about you and how he felt about fatherhood. It was always great to pass up your dad; he had this **great sense of humor**. It was weird but hilarious at the same time because he always had this straight face when he was messing with me. He told me to come by the tent to see how big you had gotten in a few months, and I told him I would. We ended up at the chow hall together, and I saw him shoveling food in his mouth, so I joked with him that there was enough food here to last a week and that he didn't have to rush. His response to me was, "Tran, I gotta be on this mission tonight, and what if I don't come back? Better to have my stomach full!" We gave him a piece of our* *mind to even joke like that—call it intuition if you want. That was his last meal.*

You remember when I said your dad was a good leader? Well, he wasn't supposed to be on this mission, but they needed someone, so he volunteered. That's how I remember your dad: **unselfish, funny and one hell of a soldier** *(excuse my language).*

I am very sorry, Miss Halie… I've held onto this for over a decade. I didn't complete my mission and your dad couldn't come home. I promise you that I would have taken his spot so that he could be with you, but that was out of my control, and it wasn't my decision to make. I'll never forget what I heard over the radio and how silent our camp was when the news came over. We were sobbing and angry. We wanted to suit up and get him ourselves. We simply couldn't do anything.

At his service, while we were in Iraq, as I saluted him for the last time, I knew this world had lost a good man, husband, and father. What is even more difficult for me to comprehend is that I felt guilty for being helpless and that you were not going to have Sgt. Van Orman. He will always be my **hero.** *I don't know if I would have been able to do what he did. He was* **brave and valiant.**

He will always be honored in my life. I am who I am today because I met a soldier like your dad. I am blessed to have a family of my own to understand and appreciate what I have because of your dad. It's been a long journey for me to get to this point to express these loving words to you about your dad.

I am sorry that none of us from the Triple Deuce can replace your dad, but we want you to know that he is your guardian angel. He is always with you as we help him keep watch over you. The small gifts you receive from time to time from your uncles at the Triple Deuce is our way of honoring him through you.

I hope when you read this letter with Mom that you don't feel sad about his loss, but I want you to be proud of what he did and how he impacted those around him. Especially me. I would like to share that he is one of our angels that we pray to in my house at night. Not a day goes by that my friend Sgt. Timothy Van Orman doesn't run through my mind. I am honored to have served with him and proud to call him my Army brother.

Maybe one day, you and I will cross paths, and I can tell him that I finally met you.

Miss Halie, I hope this note finds you well and when time gets tough that you know he's one of the stars in the sky twinkling at you.

DEEDS NOT WORDS

Respectfully,
Sgt. Hien Tran (HT) (Retired)

Since we're on the topic of seeking help and mental well-being, let me share my perspective. For us men, seeking help is not a sign of weakness, nor does it make you any less of a man. Many of us suffer in silence, fearing judgment or criticism from others. I'm done with that. We owe it to ourselves to prioritize our well-being to find happiness, love, and, most importantly, freedom. There shouldn't be a stigma around getting therapy; it's about breaking through your own walls to feel liberated, redeemed, and empowered to grow as a human being.

Part of my journey has been rebuilding my faith and learning to let go of the need to understand or solve everything in life (a challenging feat for someone with likely obsessive-compulsive tendencies—or maybe I'm just a bit rigid!). Instead, I'm learning to appreciate each moment and to be present (easier said than done)—that's been my kryptonite. Therapy helped me see things differently, helping me adjust my mindset. "Overcome and adapt" is what we were taught in the Infantry, but it's an entirely different fight when you're waging war with yourself. You feel like quitting because you're stuck in place, watching the world move on without you. Therapy has allowed me to pause, breathe, reassess my situation, and walk in a new direction.

Life no longer feels like a solo race—I've decided I'll enjoy the marathon. It won't be easy, but I'll be okay, and I know you will be too. I'll keep my faith, knowing we only get one chance at this life, and I trust that my pain isn't greater than God's love. It's taken me a long time to reach this point, but Sgt. Van Orman remains my guiding principle and the foundation of why I served. God didn't want me to forget that; He pushed me to my limits to work through it. I just have to serve in a different way, with a new perspective.

As human beings, we love to control everything around us, but some things are beyond our control or understanding. We

like to believe we have that power. I spent a good year in coun-
seling, and I am so grateful for the blessings it brought me. I've
come to accept that I did the best I could in that situation. For
the longest time, I thought it was guilt that weighed me down,
but really, it was the disappointment of not completing my
mission. It felt like another failure, yet so much larger than me.
The most critical realization I came to was that God wanted me
to forgive myself. Writing that letter to Sgt. Van Orman's
daughter was one of the hardest things I've ever done, but it
gave me perspective as a man, soldier, husband, and father and
has allowed me to connect with others on their journeys.

The letter was well-received; Mrs. Van Orman said it was
beautifully written and that it would help her daughter heal. I
know the letter was meant for their daughter, but in many ways,
it was also meant for me. It helped me process my grief. Interest-
ingly, this is the first time I've referred to it as grief. A song that
resonates with my experience of loss is Green Day's "Wake Me
Up When September Ends." The lyrics capture the passage of
time and how grief keeps our memories locked in place while
life continues. Grief is like a time capsule that can feel impos-
sible to fill until one day, you look up and realize you've missed
so many other moments. That was the lesson: Even though he
was gone, Sgt. Van Orman was never truly lost.

We honor Sgt. Van Orman by being present for our families,
by feeling grateful and blessed for all we have—the roof over
our heads, food on the table, and, most importantly, loved ones
to live for. Time doesn't heal pain; it allows you to process grief.
You heal your heart, mind, and soul when you're ready to fill in
the incompleteness with faith and peace. You honor those
you've lost by living your life to the fullest, redefining what life

looks like now. You won't be the same person you were with them, and that's okay; you'll be stronger for yourself and for them.

CHAPTER 5

"Sometimes we don't know what God is willing to do for us
until we are in a situation where only God can do it for us...
God won't walk you to what he won't walk you through..."
–DMX
(RIP, you are missed as one of the greatest
rappers of my time... top 5 easily)

L ife has handed me difficult times, yet my faith has always
been there to help me climb out of those dark moments,
whether I realized it at the time or not. It hasn't always been an
easy process to stay strong in my faith, especially when I struggled to trust the journey. But each day, my faith has grown
stronger as I understand more about the fundamentals of life
(always continuing to learn). I've learned to ask for what I need,
not simply what I want. I'm blessed to be alive and grateful for

each breath. Even in times when I felt alone and desperate, He was always there to believe in me.

Throughout my life, there were signs of God's presence on my path. Raised as a Buddhist, I made the choice to convert to Catholicism at 24. Buddhism will always be part of me, a part of my heritage, but I felt drawn to God because I needed a more personal spiritual connection. This is what I needed for myself, and I'm not criticizing others' beliefs or being judgemental. Faith is a deeply personal journey, and sometimes people may judge you for how you choose to believe. But my relationship with God is my own, and there's no room for others' judgments. I have only come this far because I serve God and honor the blessings He has provided. As a man and a soldier, I need a belief system that grounds my moral compass and guides how I engage with the world. There have been many times when I questioned my faith in humanity, and He has guided me to the light to clarify my challenges. I'm not asking God to fix me—He created me as I am—but rather to give me humility and grace to see the world through His eyes, not just my own.

My faith journey started with curiosity, a search for guidance and purpose, but it was seeded in the difficult moments when I felt I had no other options. Humbly, I knew I couldn't do this alone, and the signs were there all along; I just hadn't recognized them. Religion was always important in my family growing up, and my dad taught me to believe—but what did that really mean? As a child, we were taught to pray, but it was more of a cultural practice, a part of our Buddhist traditions. While I respected it, it felt routine, almost transactional; I didn't yet know how to find a meaningful connection.

In college, the first time I attended church, the experience planted the first seed of faith in me. It was 1997, and my fraternity brothers (props to Delta Tau Delta) would faithfully attend Spanish Mass every Sunday morning, no matter how wild the night before. Despite their hangovers, they would get up and go, honoring this one commitment. I found it peculiar, and eventually, I asked to join them; they welcomed me warmly. I remember not understanding the sermon because it was in Spanish, but I was struck by the emotional connection—the way people seemed to listen with their hearts. This moment planted a seed, though it would take years for my faith to sprout fully.

After some difficult times, including a breakup in my twenties, I found myself contemplating life in a more profound way. I knew something was missing inside me, something I couldn't quite explain at the time. That feeling of needing to search for or explore something deeper persisted, even if I didn't yet understand what it was. This wasn't a journey that happened "overnight;" it was a gradual process, a series of moments that ultimately led me to build my faith.

The place where my faith sprouted was a beautiful area in Santa Clara, CA, called "Our Lady of Peace," with a large statue of the Virgin Mary. I'd heard that the Virgin Mary, Jesus' mother, embraced those in need and that this symbolic figure had helped cure people of sickness, struggles, and losses. I was simply there to cure my heartbreak (I know it sounds silly—just bear with me). It became a place where I could be vulnerable, even in the presence of strangers. After closing down at work, I'd go there from 10 p.m. to midnight, trying to work through my feelings.

The statue meant more than just a symbol; she was like a mother figure—a role missing in my life at the time (which I won't go into here). For the first time, I could sit there and just let everything out. I would cry, talk, and just release my thoughts to someone I didn't even know or fully understand, yet it felt natural. There was an aura that made me feel protected, and I returned night after night for over six months. Soon, it became a ritual; I even started bringing friends who would sometimes just sit with me in silence. This space was good for my well-being, and my soul felt drawn to it. I began feeling lighter, as if someone else was helping carry my weight.

At that moment in my life, I was exhausted from chasing everyone else's expectations. I was trying hard to get back on track and make a plan for my future. The hardest part was figuring out what I would do now that I had finally graduated college (in 2003). That journey alone had been a challenge, but reaching that milestone didn't mean much—I graduated with a 2.0 GPA. The question loomed: What's next? Everything felt mundane.

I distinctly remember one day standing outside and asking God for a sign. The conversation in my heart was something like this: "I'm not of your faith, but you seem to listen and accept me as I visit this church often. I come to Mother Mary and unload, but I get the sense she wants me to come talk with you. God, just give me a sign. I've been here for a while, and I don't know what it means to be Catholic. I don't even understand the kind of relationship I'm supposed to have with you, but I keep showing up." Sometimes, you just have to throw a Hail Mary and see what happens, especially if you've got nothing else in your arsenal.

Then, a sign came. One day, stress got to me: the voices of insecurity and the infatuation of trying to prove I am worthy caused an irritability in my mind and heart, seeing everyone else with a clear path to their future. It was overwhelming, and I started spiraling mentally. I needed a break. I felt sick. I told my boss, a dear friend, that I needed a few hours and would return to help close the store. It was midday, and I decided to break my routine, something I'd been rigidly maintaining as I was learning to set better boundaries. I went to Our Lady of Peace, and something unique happened.

I was sitting on a bench at the church, praying, or more like having a conversation. A mass had just ended, and people were milling around. I started tearing up, and soon, I was sobbing. I could not hold onto the tidal waves of emotions at this point… it came on so suddenly. Maybe it was not as sudden as I believe it to be… but it was the right time for the emotions to be released. At some point, I looked up and saw a little old lady. She was petite, with a gentle voice, and she said, "Hey, I noticed you've been sitting here. Let me give you this." She handed me a rosary, crafted in a style similar to Buddhist prayer beads worn on the wrist. I looked at it and thanked her. "Ma'am, I'm not even Catholic; I don't even know how to use this," I said.

She replied, "It's okay; you can just hold onto it. When you need to pray, just hold the beads, okay?"

I nodded, replying, "Yes, ma'am," as I sat there, feeling everything all at once. The release of emotion was like releasing the dam for the water to flow (Yes, I have feelings—even if we men don't always like to admit it, they exist.)

And then she walked off. I looked at the beads in my hand, feeling a mix of curiosity and a bit of disbelief. Why would someone just randomly give me something like this out of nowhere? My initial reaction felt a bit ungrateful—I was questioning why someone would give me something for nothing. Nothing in life is truly free; free for me, maybe, but it costs someone something (Economics 101—I did pay attention to that). I thought, what am I supposed to do with this? Then, my manners kicked in, and I felt rude for not even expressing gratitude for the gesture. I got up to look for her, scanning the area.

I looked around, but she was nowhere to be found. Mass had just let out, so there were about 40 to 50 people scattered in front of the church and around the statue. The woman had been in her late '70s or '80s, petite and easy to spot, but she had vanished. I was sure it had been less than a minute since she'd given me the beads—there was no way she could have walked away that quickly. (I still get goosebumps when I tell people this story.)

I'm known for being a fast walker, and I searched the area at least three times, but she was nowhere in sight. I thought, *Was that a sign?* I don't know what it was, but it felt like an angel answered my call. There's more to the story of those beads, but I'll get to that later. That moment shook me deeply.

One of my close friends, Pat Nocero Jr.—also known as "Seagull" (the guy could eat all day without gaining a pound)—went to church every Sunday without fail. I worked up the courage to ask him about his faith, which felt awkward because I wasn't used to talking about religion. I said, "Hey Pat, would you mind if I asked you a weird question?"

He looked at me and said, "Sure, what's up?"

I asked, "Would you mind if I tagged along with you to church one of these days? I've been sitting outside of this church, and I want to go in, but I'm nervous about offending anyone or feeling out of place. I'm Buddhist, after all."

Pat said, "No problem. I'll talk to my mom, and we'll set it up."

The Nocero family is truly incredible. Pat's mom, Beverly, is one of the kindest, most compassionate people I've ever met, especially when it comes to her love for God and the Holy Spirit.

She's like a fireball of Italian warmth and energy. I was invited to join them, and that connection became one of the most meaningful relationships in my life. Mama Nocero eventually became my godmother and my spiritual compass. (I love you, Mama.)

Mama took me to church, and when I was there, I felt something. I felt a sense of belonging, as if I were meant to be in His home. I kept that feeling to myself because I didn't want to rush it. I listened intently to the sermon, and it felt as though the words were meant for me. The message was about feeling lost and finding your way home, about how it was okay to stray as long as you remembered where home was. It touched my heart, and I found myself tearing up. The essence of the sermon was, "Come back home to me; we'll work through this together. Trust me to do my work." It was as though God was saying, "You're protected here, not judged. I'm here for you."

Grateful for the experience, I started returning. No one pressured me or had expectations. This was entirely my decision. I remember asking Mama Nocero, "How will I know when I'm ready?"

She replied, "God has always been ready to accept you. You just have to open up and accept Him."

I believe everyone's relationship with God is different. For me, it's like talking to my best friend—there's no pretense. If you know me, you know my conversations are full of interesting things and sometimes a few F-bombs. Some people may not agree with that, but it doesn't matter—it's my relationship with God, not theirs. In those conversations, I'm just grateful for the essentials: God, country, family, a roof over my head, food on the table, and love and compassion for myself and others (always a work in progress).

Then came a pivotal moment. I had struggled for so long

with how people viewed me and how I allowed their opinions to affect me. Finally, I understood that God didn't create me to be judged by others—only by Him. He is my Creator. I committed to being baptized and aligning my values with His teachings. It's a continuous journey, but I'm learning. My godparents, Beverly and Patrick (Sr.) Nocero, have been a huge blessing in my life. When I first returned to the U.S. after being injured in Iraq, my godparents were the first people I saw at Walter Reed Medical Center, smiling and telling me I would be alright. They truly are my living angels. (I love you, Mama and Papa.) This was the first sign I recognized as God's blessing to help me continue my journey.

The second sign came in the process of my decision to enlist in the Army. At this stage in my life, I was trying to be more intentional about my career and where I wanted to go. I had been working in Loss Prevention at Macy's for four years and had been testing for multiple police departments without success. California was going through an energy and financial crisis from 2003 to 2005, and although I made it to the San Jose Police Department Chief's interview twice, the academy shut down both times. I was always inches from the finish line but never crossed it. My last shot was to transfer my testing package for a recruit position at another academy—a rare opportunity during those tough economic times. All I had to do was pass an obstacle course. The final obstacle was a 6-foot wall, and as I jumped over it and started the final 100-meter sprint, my right knee popped twice, and I collapsed. Crawling to the finish line wasn't enough; the facilitator had already disqualified me, and paramedics were on the way.

The recovery went relatively quickly, but it took five months of therapy to feel back to normal. Once again, I found myself asking, *What now?* I felt burnt out from running in circles with no clear direction. My godmother had always told me to let go of my desire to control everything and to trust in God. But I constantly found myself trying to steer things, haunted by the time I felt I'd wasted in the past. I prayed, asking God what He wanted me to do next. The pursuit of becoming a police officer had run into countless roadblocks, and I felt as if I were being nudged in another direction. I thought about the conversation I mentioned earlier in the book: about what people would say about us if we died today. Everything seemed to be pointing me toward something bigger than myself. I prayed again, asking, "Is the military the right path for me? And if so, which branch?" This was my trust exercise, and I was nervous. By the end of that prayer, though, I had made my decision: I was going to enlist.

If you've ever been in a military recruiting center, you know they're usually bustling. That day, I asked my boss for an extended lunch break, planning to make up the time by closing the store later. I wasn't ready to tell anyone because I didn't want anyone talking me out of it. I sat in my car in the parking lot, asking God to guide me to the right branch.

My family had a proud Navy tradition from southern Vietnam. A year after 9/11, my brother enlisted in the Marine Corps, becoming the first in our generation to continue our family's military tradition. In the car, I prayed, saying, "Whoever grabs me first is the branch I'll join." As I entered the building off Almaden Expressway, it was unusually quiet. I passed the Air Force office, where a sign read *"Downsizing."* The Marine Corps office was closed (odd for a Thursday afternoon), and the Coast Guard office was closed as well. The Navy office was packed with recruits who didn't notice me (which was fine; it wasn't my first choice). Then, there was the Army office at the end of the hall. It was empty except for one staff sergeant gazing outside. My heart was pounding, and my stomach was tied in knots. I took a deep breath and asked if he could help me.

I only remember his last name, Staff Sergeant Lei. He asked about my education, and I told him I was a college graduate. He shook his head, saying, "Wrong office; try Sunnyvale for Officer Candidate School (OCS)."

As he started to walk away, I stopped him, saying, "No sir, I'm in the right place. I don't want to go to OCS. I want to enlist, and I want to join the Infantry."

He chuckled, looking me up and down, probably thinking I was crazy. But after I explained that I wanted to start from the bottom and work my way up—so I could learn and earn my way rather than be handed a position—I finally convinced him to help me enlist.

This wasn't about me. This was about my purpose, a purpose I felt God had given me: to serve others. The idea of earning my way up appealed to me; it felt right, making me feel determined and accountable for once. I trusted the process and believed in the path God was setting before me. No regrets. "God loves the Infantry!" (*wink*—for my Infantry brothers).

The third blessing He gave me was life and a new perspective. I'm still figuring it all out, and I'm grateful for every lesson along the way. Let me ask you this: Is your faith based on coincidences, or do you believe in miracles? I think you know my answer. To me, everything—every blessing—is a miracle because I'm not owed or entitled to anything. I'm indebted to my experiences for the lessons they've given me about serving Him and learning more about myself. This third blessing completely changed who I am, and I'm still discovering who that is. I believe God had a plan for me.

One of the most common questions I get asked is: "Do you regret joining the Army?" I don't believe in regret. Decisions are founded on the values and beliefs we hold at that time. Everything happens for a reason, and the lessons that come from those experiences are invaluable. What you do with that value is entirely up to you, based on the impact you want to make.

––––––

The moment I'm about to share is a combination of my own memories and details recalled by those who were with me that night. Some parts are a bit "blurry"—no pun intended.

On Mother's Day 2008 (May 10), while in Iraq, we were assigned to support a special operations team that operated under different procedures than ours—Task Force 17, nicknamed "Ghost." We had been supporting this team for almost six months, including training and living alongside them on missions. It was one of the most intense and exciting things I'd ever done. We switched from daytime to nighttime missions, often lasting anywhere from a day to a week, depending on the objectives and needs.

The day before the mission, we received a briefing, and I felt something wasn't right, though I couldn't put my finger on it. This wasn't our usual type of 24-hour mission, and it felt a bit rushed to me. The last time we'd had a 24-hour mission, if I remember correctly, was with Sgt. Van Orman. There was something unsettling about the intel we received. I'm pretty sure I voiced my concerns to someone. I thought it was my captain, but he doesn't recall the conversation. I definitely went back to my squad and told them to be ready for exfil (exfiltration) later that night.

After the debrief, I went back to my tent. Normally, I'd return, give my team their rundown on what we needed in terms of ammo and supplies, and make sure our communication gear was set. I was the radio telephone operator (RTO) and also part of a Weapons Squad. I briefed my team so they could prepare their weapons, ammo, and the other equipment we'd need. But something felt off to me. My squad picked up on it and asked what was wrong. I shared my thoughts, and they brushed it off, saying, "Tran, you're overthinking this. We'll be back in time for morning chow. In and out."

I told them to "f-off" in the most affectionate way possible, as only brothers can. It almost felt like a scene from *Black Hawk Down* when the team is getting ready to go out. My team tried to negotiate with me about carrying a lighter load, but I wasn't having it, which led to the usual, "Old man, you worry too much." For context, I was 27 at the time. To them, though, I was practically ancient—probably the fourth oldest in the platoon after my platoon sergeant and a couple of squad leaders.

My usual pre-mission ritual involved blasting some old-school hip hop, like Ice Cube or DMX, to get my adrenaline going and saying a prayer to Saint Michael, my patron saint, and Jesus. But that day, there was no adrenaline. Instead, I listened to '90s R&B and found myself looking through my family photo album—a personal taboo. I just knew in my gut that something was going to go wrong.

One of my younger soldiers asked, "So, should we only carry about a thousand rounds today?"

My response was a firm "No way." For reference, on the weapons team, every 100 rounds adds about seven pounds due to the machine gun we carried. Carrying 1,000 rounds is about 70 pounds, and that's considered a light load for us. I told them,

"You need to carry between 3,000 to 5,000 rounds per gun." They weren't happy, but I added, "We're bringing everything as if this mission will last five or six days," and I had already confirmed this with our squad leader.

Hours later, when I left that tent, I knew I wouldn't see it again. When we landed at one in the morning, everything on the intel sheet was wrong. Nothing matched what we had planned for, and the drop-off by the "birds" was rough as we stumbled out. Someone spotted a house flickering in the distance that wasn't on our map. Our nearest support, the 2nd and 3rd Platoons from Anvil Company, were over a klick out, and our air assets, which were supposed to monitor us from above, had to refuel. We were out there alone. We needed to breach that house quickly, but the map didn't show any ravines, and it was a few hundred meters away. We had to proceed carefully. We held our position on the main road as we worked things out.

We had been on this road for a while when we finally got the orders to move. That was the "moment." I remember a huge, bright blast as I turned my head to gather my element after my captain gave the orders. It was only seconds but felt like an eternity. Everything after that is mostly a mystery to me.

One thing I'm sure of: There was a silhouette, incredibly bright, shaped like a person but without a distinguishable face. As I lay on the ground, it was just me and this figure. It was so quiet and serene—I didn't feel any pain; I just felt worn out. I assumed it was God, thinking I was done, not knowing what had happened after the blast. I remember having a conversation. "God, I'm exhausted. If it's my time to go, I'll follow you faithfully, no questions asked. But if it's not my time... I've done everything I wanted in my life; I think I've experienced enough

99

in this lifetime. But there's one thing I haven't found—I haven't found love or fallen in love…" Then, there was only silence.

The next thing I knew, I was awake in a hospital at Balad Air Force Base. My captain and I were both severely injured. He lost his leg, and I lost my right eye and injured my leg. We had been hit by an IED (improvised explosive device). It took me 15 months to recover from my injuries, with countless months of rehabilitation. When my captain and I were sent back to the States, Anvil Company had to continue their missions. I was anxious for them to return because I had so many questions about that night—the night that redefined my perspective in life.

One of my biggest frustrations was trying to understand why I was alive and what my purpose was… again. But I needed to know more details to make sense of it all. Months later, when the unit finally arrived back at Fort Drum, New York, I was eager to reunite with Anvil Company and my platoon. The person I most wanted to see was our medic, Doc Cody Williams, who patched me up. I missed him and my brothers, especially my squad. I visited them, and it was incredible to see everyone again. While I was catching up with Doc Williams, he handed me a Ziploc bag that I instantly recognized. I asked him where he got it.

He asked me, "Did you throw this out when you fell? We found it about ten feet away from you."

I replied, "How would I have had time to reach into my uniform shirt—covered by my Kevlar vest and my weapon strapped across my chest—to pull it out before the blast?"

Inside the bag were my prayer cards of Saint Michael, a picture of my grandmother, and the rosary beads given to me at the church. I froze, my heart pounding so loudly I could hear it. Once I heard his explanation, I didn't share anything further with anyone else. I only had more questions: *Why me? Why was I kept alive? What was my purpose?* It was too overwhelming to process at that moment, but I knew this: I was a survivor, not a victim.

Fifteen months of recovery left me feeling angry. My family and friends will tell you that anger has kept me going. They say I'm like a miniature version of the Incredible Hulk. I couldn't answer these questions, but I knew I was blessed with a second chance. I was a mix of emotions. If I count up all the times I've come close to death, I feel like a cat with nine lives, but this incident hit the hardest. I had my ups and downs trying to make sense of it all. I was also frustrated with the feeling of incompletion—once again, I hadn't fulfilled my objective of sending a soldier home safely for them to be with their families. The one purpose I'd set for myself when I enlisted. Now, I was the one heading home. I know it might sound ungrateful, but I felt like I was starting over and, once more, running in circles.

———

This second chance at life feels like winning the lottery—it won't happen again... I might even consider this my third chance after what had happened in college. It took me a long time to understand all the questions I was asking. I know I was trying to control the situation, but He was not allowing that. God gives you what you need, not what you want. I had to stop, but I didn't know how. I decided to approach this one day at a time. I'm not backing down from anything—I will fight through this with every breath I have. This became my new perspective. I learned to embrace the challenge. I'll go 12 rounds with anyone and won't even care if I lose—but you're going to remember me. I won't go down easy anymore.

Your opportunity in this world is a privilege, not a right, and He reminds you not to waste it. I choose to see it that way because you're measured by what your character does in times of adversity and by how strong your will truly is, using that strength to impact others. This is my God, who Himself went through trials and tribulations to give His life so that I could live.

My faith has helped me understand that my journey isn't perfect, and that's okay. I just needed to find and understand the fighter in me. I use my faith to strengthen myself and those around me, to accept who we are in the moment so we can build into who we need to be. It's not always about the end result—it's about the journey. When I struggle in this life, that's when God is most present, helping me reflect and understand the situation from a different perspective.

I believe God sends people into our lives who guide us and help us grow our faith. We all experience pain, and that pain can carry lessons that can help others. I believe that. We go through trials and tribulations so we can appreciate and be grateful for what we have. As I end this chapter, I'm reminded of the lyrics of a song by DMX: "Lord, give me a sign. Amen, Lord, give me a sign. I really need to talk to you, Lord. Since the last time we talked, the walk has been hard. Now, I know you haven't left me, but I feel like I'm alone. I'm a big boy now, but I'm still not grown."

It's an ongoing process that will continue until our last breath. That's our connection to God, to who and where we are in life. All that I have in my life today isn't because of what I did; it's because of what God has blessed me with. And the most important gift He gave me was a second chance to see life from a different perspective. I used to fear death, but I no longer do. Death is my friend, waiting to accompany me to Him. This life does not belong to me anymore; it belongs to Him who I serve. I look forward to answering God's question about what I've done to impact this world when my time is called. Yet, there is still more work to do.

CHAPTER 6

*"What would you do, if I sang out of tune? Would you stand up
and walk out on me? Lend me your ears and I'll sing
you a song, I will try not to sing out of key."*
–Joe Cocker "With a Little Help from My Friends"
(theme song for *The Wonder Years*)

S ome people believe in love at first sight, and some of us
chase it our whole lives and never find it. Some of us run
from it until we stumble and fall and then find "the one." Love
is a perception—there are so many ways to look at it that sometimes it's right there, and we choose not to see it. Love is more
than just romance; we often focus on that because of what we
see in movies and the media. I believe love has many layers and
complexities, which is what makes it special. Love also changes

and is defined by our life experiences. The most unconditional love is the way you love yourself. Sometimes, we look in the mirror and aren't true to who we are because we're chasing something that doesn't reflect us, thinking it's love—a change that happens in an instant.

I think we all have a definition of love that reflects others but not ourselves, and it becomes difficult to accept who we are, so we change on others' behalf. That's important to talk about because when we discuss love in a general sense, it's always about loving someone else. But no one really teaches you how to love yourself.

For men especially, love involves sacrifices and vulnerability that we don't always talk about or feel comfortable with. I'm the same way. These are all the "feelings" we keep inside and never show the world, which becomes exhausting. A man's first love is his mother, and that is the foundation and principle of his love and trust.

Our father's love is the foundation and principle of account-ability and commitment to who we want to be as a man. One is an *internal* perception, and the other is an *external* perception. Both are very important, and if one is compromised, it can set off our internal compass. For many men, love means sacrificing and exposing our emotions, but mostly, it's about trust. It's not easy to give, especially for those of us who grew up in a different era, culture, or environment from the "norm." Love was shown through action, not words. Love was in fulfilling responsibilities, providing for, and protecting our families. That's how men showed love—as part of their duty. That kind of love is sacrifice. As men, we carry that weight on our shoulders proudly but often suffer in silence, so everyone assumes we're doing fine. Who loves that man enough to check on him? This was the example I learned from my dad. I saw it my whole life.

Love is an evolution, and we redefine it as we go through life. It isn't always portrayed realistically because it ages, and it's more than just passion or compassion in the moment. You have to be in tune with your emotions and values. Is love patient? Is love forgiving? Is it security? Is it comfort? Love isn't always about people; I think it starts with our faith and builds from there. My definition of true love is forgiving, accepting, and understanding the other person (which is something I have to work on daily for myself and is a work in progress). This has been redefined many times, and this is my current perspective. To be honest, I'm not always good at it. I struggle very much with forgiveness, especially with forgiving myself. Sometimes we're disappointed when we give too much, and it's not returned. The way we learn love shapes our relationships with loved ones, as partners and parents, and in our relationship with God.

Early on, love wasn't something I understood or accepted, especially with myself. I'm tough on who I am today because of the mistakes I made when I was younger. For most of my adolescence, love was shown by having a roof over our heads, food on the table, and clothes on our backs. My dad's love was shown through food, and that bond has always stayed with me. But we never heard the words "I love you." It wasn't part of our culture, and I don't blame my dad because it wasn't his custom. As an American kid, if you don't get that at home, you seek it elsewhere, looking for instant gratification rather than true meaning. My brother and I knew he loved us, but it was always tough love. He would reprimand us but always had our backs, no matter how foolish the decisions we made growing up.

Now, at 45, he still checks in on me to make sure I'm okay and that my family is well. The first time I ever heard my dad say, "I love you, son," was at my Army boot camp graduation when he was pinning on my blue Infantry cord. Since I had skipped a college graduation, I felt I owed him some kind of ceremony. I remember standing at attention as families came into formation, and when he stood in front of me for the first time, I felt he was proud of me. I wasn't a boy in his eyes anymore but a man. Then he said it, and let me tell you, there was a big "frog" in my throat that I could hardly hold back. I realized I'd been waiting for that moment a long time to make him proud—a pride he had always felt, even if I hadn't believed it.

I never fully understood parental love until I became a parent myself. When my firstborn came into our lives, everything my dad had done for me suddenly made sense, and I knew I'd do the same for my own son and daughter. I am blessed with two amazing kids: Clayton and Annabelle. They're incredibly special to me, and having them has shifted my entire perspective on life and driven me to be better. (I love you, my guy, and I love you, my forever daddy's little girl.) With children, that "love" reaches a new level; you'd do anything and everything to make sure they're okay. I don't live my life just for myself anymore—I live it for them. I find myself saying and doing things my dad would do for me. My love language, like his, is also through food, and I've passed that down to my son and daughter. One of my dad's comforts was cooking for us whenever he sensed I was unwell or just having a rough day. He'd whip up a bowl of noodles from scratch with whatever ingredients we had. My favorite was his egg noodles with stir-fried cabbage—so simple but made with love.

One of the most amusing and frustrating things to see now is how soft my dad has gotten as a grandparent. He won't even raise his voice with my kids! The rule used to be, "You eat what I cook, no questions asked." A few years ago, he came to visit me in Texas for a week and would cook meals for us each day. One day, he spent hours in the kitchen making duck salad with rice porridge (one of my favorite dishes). My son walked by, saw the meal, and made a face. My dad decided the meal wasn't good enough for his grandson, so he went back to the kitchen to make spaghetti just to make him happy. I stopped, annoyed, and told him, "My son will eat what you cooked."

But my dad shook his head, saying, "If he doesn't like duck, I'll make spaghetti so he can enjoy it."

I barely recognized the man standing in front of me! I asked, "What happened to 'You eat what I cook?'"

He replied, "That only applies to you." (This entire exchange was in Vietnamese, of course.) Suddenly, he's a grandfather, and the rules apparently don't apply anymore! (Cue eye roll.)

One of the greatest blessings God gave me was love after my injuries, which was something I hadn't understood well before joining the Army. I had always tried to fill a void in my heart, but no one ever could. I looked for it, but in the end, I was the one standing in my own way. When it comes to love, trust is essential, and my biggest fear is being abandoned. I have experienced that in my life. For my brother and me, we were lucky, our dad was the stable and consistent pillar in our lives. I acknowledge that this is more than what some others have, and I am blessed and grateful for that. His love was "tough love," but as young men growing up, we needed it.

In my personal life, I'd often connect quickly with "the ladies," but I always kept them at arm's length. My real issue was that I couldn't trust people. That foundation was broken for me, and it made it very difficult for me to be open and honest to let someone in. As soon as I felt I was starting to develop feelings, I'd find an exit or an excuse because my expectations—and fears—would change. That was my love life: I'd start something, then bail when it became serious, always running from the possibility of being abandoned. I loved the chase, especially when I couldn't get what I wanted. It fed my insecurities. The longest relationship in my young adult life was about three years. She was ready to move forward, but I got so scared of the commitment that I broke up with her, too afraid to let someone in to help me heal.

Looking back, I was never ready to commit to anyone. I loved the idea of it, but it was unrealistic for me. Some might have seen me as a "player," but I wasn't that cool. I was just running away from people, hurting a few along the way, which I regret. And there were a few who broke my heart, which only cemented me further in my non-committal ways, hurting even those who truly cared about me.

I hadn't been able to define what love truly meant for me. As I was "maturing," I realized it wasn't just about the physical side. I needed to feel safe in a relationship—where I could be myself, vulnerabilities and all, without judgment. While in the service, my rule was not to commit to anyone because I'd seen the hardship of saying goodbye when it was time to deploy. I knew this going in, but that didn't stop me from playing the field. And as they say, when you play with fire, you eventually get burned.

Growing up, I imagined my love life would be like *The Wonder Years*, wanting that pure love Kevin Arnold had for Winnie Cooper—even if, in the end, they didn't make it. Yes, I'm a proud nerd. Kevin and I had a lot in common: We didn't know what we wanted, and we were more focused on making others happy than ourselves. This is what I meant when I started this chapter: We often define love based on someone else's view of us rather than being true to ourselves. I believe in compromise, but not at the cost of losing who I am. And sure, there was a time in my 20s when I wanted to "be a baller, shot caller, twenty-inch blades on the Impala," as the song goes (thanks, Lil' Troy). I was none of those things, EVER—but back then, I would've told you otherwise, especially when I was trying to impress someone. It was always about the perception that I wanted to give but never about who I truly was.

When I asked God for love as I lay there, thinking I was taking my last breath, I didn't really know what I was asking for. With my injuries, I knew my insecurities would grow. Who was going to love a guy with one eye? If I couldn't accept myself, how could I expect anyone else to? I carried a lot of emotional baggage but kept it all inside because that's what men do—or so I thought. The one thing I forgot to lean on was my faith: to help me heal and eventually learn to love myself.

I truly believe God works in mysterious ways. My wife, Nadine, and I had been friends for a long time, even before I enlisted. We met through a mutual best friend and would see each other whenever I was on leave, hanging out with the "crew." We were always friendly and a little flirty, but it was never serious. (For the record, she was much more flirtier than I was...wink) While I was in the hospital, I heard her mother was unwell, so I sent flowers as a gesture of compassion. Sadly, her mother passed shortly afterward.

It's interesting that my relationship with Nadine started with a question about death. I had been given a new lease on life, and she'd lost someone she loved—a feeling I could relate to. A few weeks later, I checked in on her. I was curious about how she felt about loss. I was still grappling with my own emotions over Sgt. Van Orman and my Ba Noi. I was angry with God but also grateful for what He'd done for me. It was the most confusing time of my life—a "hot mess," as they say. I asked her, "Are you mad at God for taking your mother away?"

She replied, "No. I miss her, but I'm not angry. She's no longer in pain, and the Lord took her to end her suffering. That gives me comfort."

That answer alone reserved a part of my heart for Nadine. Something in me knew she could be "the one." We ended up talking for almost three hours that night.

When I finally made it home after retiring a year later, we started dating. (I'll fast-forward a bit; you don't need the "steamy" details—LOL.) Nadine helped me learn to trust and love. She wasn't afraid to be blunt with me and always kept it real. Before we were officially dating, we went to a bar for a birthday party, and someone shoved me. Without hesitation, she defended me on the spot. I knew then she was my "ride or die."

But it wasn't always easy for her. I don't make things easy. Our love isn't perfect, but we keep fighting for it. My rigid ways, anxiety, and tendency for "fight or flight" haven't helped. I trust her to have my back, but there were times I wasn't there for her. Like many men, I was good at bottling things up instead of expressing them. Nadine, on the other hand, is intuitive with her emotions. I'd build everything up, then explode like a bomb. The only emotion she would see from me was anger, which was unfair to her. I'd always say, "Everything is okay," sweeping things under the rug—but was it really? It never was until I blew up and had "my moment."

And then it's like ground zero again. How much more could she endure?

My wife has been my emotional coach, you could say. We've been married for 14 years now, and I'm gradually becoming more comfortable with the idea of expressing my feelings. I'm getting better at it, not that I'm necessarily good at it yet. I tend to get defensive because I feel judged, and that's my issue. I supposedly don't care... but, truth be told, I really do. Our marriage isn't picture-perfect (but who's is)—there's always room for improvement—but she holds me accountable for my actions, reactions, and considerations. Actually, we hold each other accountable for our actions. Part of this love is showing our kids a healthy, honest relationship—one that isn't always perfect in what we go through as individuals or as a couple. I'm raising a young man and a little girl who need to understand what love truly is. We are their first example of that, but we also need to show them how to love themselves and recognize their own worth in a world that begins with them.

I am dedicating this chapter to my wife, Nadine, because she is my foundation of trust. She's supported me through everything—from working on my combat issues to starting a business to moving our family to Texas. I love her because she loves me for me (which is not an easy task), with all my quirks and issues, and definitely not for my looks (LOL). We are an odd couple: she's tall, I'm short; she's emotionally in tune, I'm learning; she's very outgoing, and I'm a bit of a hermit. But we complement each other. She is my rock, the one I lean on when I feel small and dismissed by the world. I'm not invincible, but with her, I feel safe. I may not show it all the time, but it's only "home" because she's there. When I say God has blessed me with her, I really mean it. Nothing in life is permanent, but I am grateful that, in this borrowed time, I get to experience this love. Perfection isn't the goal—growth in love is.

I believe true love is a marathon, not a race. So often, we get caught up in the intensity of new feelings and want everything immediately. But then reality sets in, and we meet the real person behind that initial impression. Sometimes, people give up, saying, "This isn't what I was in love with." I think this is because we see love as a sprint rather than a long, steady journey. Forget about reaching the finish line; let's focus on the journey and growth that happens along the way, which is what really matters in getting to the end together.

She has never given up on me; we've come close at times, but we've both grown together. I love you, Nadine Tran. I want you to know that I appreciate you. I wouldn't be writing this book without you and your belief and support. Thank you for helping me re-establish my pillar of trust and I want the world to know how amazing you are. There is no success in my life without you. Thank you for walking with me through this life. Thank you for loving me, even when I'm not perfect, and for being patient with me. I am a better man because of you. I dedicate Musiq's song "Don't Change" to you: "Don't you know, you'll always be the most beautiful woman I know. So let me reassure you, darling, that my feelings are truly unconditional... understand that you're all I want and need."

I've also been blessed with brotherly love. As I've grown older, I've realized that I don't need "friends"—I need my brothers. Either you're family, or you're an acquaintance. Friends come with the work of maintenance and expectations, but family doesn't. And family doesn't always mean blood relatives. Many of the people who have been there for me have been outside of my blood family. With brothers, you pick up right where you left off, even if time has passed in between. If you need them, they're there—no questions asked. I don't have to be the "tough guy" or the "cool guy" around them; I just have to be me. It's too exhausting to keep up a persona that society has cast on us. We are just human beings, like everyone else. We accept each other as we are and back each other up through hard times. These relationships are intentional, not trans-actional.

As I get older, I value the bonds of camaraderie more than ever. It's no longer about quantity but about the quality of the brotherhood. Accountability and integrity are how we show love and support. Recently, I've started breaking the taboo of talking about men's health, especially mental health. Times have changed, and we as men must do too. We have to take better care of each other, just like my brothers-in-arms once did for me. It's not about being "soft;" if I'm going to call you my "brother," then I'd better put those words into action. We are stronger as a pack than we are alone. This one is for my Bean Bag brothers and all the brothers who have been there through my hard times. I want you all to know that I appreciate and love every single one of you. It has been my honor to have you on my journey through life.

Especially my brother Hoa, my favorite Marine, who always has my back. The kid's a fighter and as stubborn as they come. Apparently, the men in the Tran family just keep fighting through life, handling whatever's thrown at us, and we are doing alright. We've been through dark times and come back from them, always moving forward. Nobody knows how to get under each other's skin like we do. We have our moments, but if anyone messes with him... I'm coming for you. It's practically my duty to piss him off (LOL). Life has thrown everything at my kid brother, yet, just like a Marine, he keeps charging forward. I'm proud of you, my brother.

Faith is a part of my love because God has blessed me far more than I deserve. True love isn't about expecting anything in return; when we do expect something, it becomes a transaction. When I look at my love for God, I ask myself: *Am I being transactional? Do I pray because I want something from Him, or do I pray because I'm grateful for what He's teaching me and the experiences He's given me?* I believe true love is unconditional, just as God's love has been with me. Love can be patience, understanding, and forgiveness. But love is also something else—it can hurt, knock you off your feet, and turn your world upside down. It's that part of love that many want to ignore, calling it by other names, but getting through those trials makes love graceful, even in its flaws. This is what separates us and builds connections that complement each other. It's the growth we seek in love. But none of that can happen if you don't accept who you are and allow others to be a part of that journey. That was my biggest struggle—the imaginary wall I built for myself until I found faith in God and met my wife, who helped me slowly tear it down.

Love is different for everyone, and there's no single standard. It's a journey and a process with many layers and perspectives. What does each of those layers mean to you in a particular relationship? Love is more than just the bond between two people; it's also about the community of people who support you through life. One thing I hope to share in this chapter is to make sure we express our appreciation for those we love before it's too late. But before you love others, learn to be grateful to yourself. Invest the time to understand and love yourself first. It sounds easy, but we often beat ourselves up more than we allow others to do. Build faith in God so that you can build faith in people, aligning the trust and expectations you have for one another. This book is my love letter to God. He has been there for me, and His relentless love has guided me. Most importantly, God has helped me learn how to love myself and accept who He has created me to be, and I continue to give Him all the glory. I am forever grateful for this experience.

CHAPTER 7

"Lean on me when you're not strong, and I'll be your friend.
I'll help you carry on. Please swallow your pride, for no one
can fill those of your needs that you won't let show."
–Bill Withers

I believe it takes a village to raise a child, and it takes a community of people to walk through life successfully. Even the word *success* evolves depending on where I am in life and who is there to guide me. As you've read, there has always been someone who believed in me more than I believed in myself. I am forever grateful for the community that raised me and for those I met along the way. Some people have been with me the whole time, while others joined for part of the journey. I don't believe in coincidences. I believe God puts certain people in your life to guide you to the next part of your path.

Sometimes success is defined by wealth or assets, but I see success as more than that. Success, to me, is a perception—more specifically, a self-perception of how well you define your life. I define success by what I've done and whom I've impacted. This is my second chance at life, and I'm on "borrowed time." When my time comes, I'll be ready to go without question, knowing I was fortunate enough to come back and learn, grow, and serve others with God's blessings. It's rare to "win the lottery" twice. When Death comes for me, I hope to tell God I did better this time than I did the first go around. We only fear Death because we think it is here to shorten or steal our time; we forget that our time was always limited from the start. We don't always remember that. As I've said before, Death is my friend, waiting to take me to see Him.

Before I go, I want certain people to know how much I appreciate them. Too often, we move through life taking from others without acknowledging the impact they've had on us. This is my opportunity to express that appreciation. Some of those people are mentioned in this book, but others may not be, and it does not mean they are any less valued.

My perspective has changed. I used to think I had to climb the mountain alone to reach the top, but I was wrong. When you reach the top by yourself, people see you as a target to tear down, and there's no one to celebrate with. But when you climb with those who helped you along the way, it's a celebration you share together. That's all that matters because their faith in me, alongside God's faith, gives me strength and purpose.

My dad is my hero. He doesn't know it, and he probably wouldn't accept it if I told him. I recently watched a movie called *The Wild Robot* by DreamWorks. *Spoiler alert:* In this movie, a robot is stranded on an island and finds a duckling to raise.

The robot, despite knowing nothing about the environment, commits to teaching the duckling how to swim and fly so it can thrive. That robot is like my dad. (I don't mean in a negative manner.) He sacrificed so much for my brother and me in a country he knew nothing about. Two different generations, two different cultures, two different perspectives—but always one heart because he is our heart.

One memory of my dad's dedication brings me to tears. When I was in the hospital, helpless and hooked up to machines with my hands bandaged, adjusting to having only one eye and coping with the pain, I hadn't been able to use the bathroom for 27 days. The doctors told me I'd need a procedure if I couldn't relieve myself soon. I was frustrated, angry, and overwhelmed, and my dad tried to comfort me, waiting until my captain, who was recovering on the other side of the room, was resting to save me some embarrassment.

My dad looked at me and asked, "What do you want to do, son?"

I said, "I don't want to go down there, Dad."

So he asked how much time we had, and they told us we had until the end of the day to resolve it. "Don't worry, son, I'm here for you," he said. He grabbed a tub from the shower and lifted me like a baby, placing me over the container. (*Sorry… frog in my throat.*) He said, "Push, son, and I'll hold you up."

I replied, "No, I can't do it, Dad."

He looked at me with such determination. "We can do this together, no matter how painful it is."

I was more embarrassed than anything—that as a grown man, I needed my dad's help with something so basic. The pain was unbearable, and I was muttering and squeezing his hand as I pushed through. My stomach was full; the smell was terrible, and there was blood in the stool. He stood by me the whole time, unwavering, not flinching once until I was done. It's not an easy story for me to tell, but it shows his reverence, sacrifice, and commitment. *(Deep sigh.)* That's the unconditional love of my father.

One of the best memories I have is cooking with my dad in the kitchen. Through cooking, he'd teach me how to plan, prepare, and then execute, just as he did every time he cooked. He was known as the master chef in our little community, especially among my friends. They'd come over excited for his food. Cooking was how he bonded with people; food was truly his love language.

Recently, we took him out for his birthday, a special steakhouse dinner with our families. I remember him sitting there, looking down at the table, glancing over at my son, my daughter, and my nephew. Then, he started to tear up. "I'm sorry, son," he said.

My brother and I were confused. "What are you talking about, Dad?"

He continued, "I feel like I failed you. I was so focused on providing for you that I never really connected. I never checked in to see how you were feeling or what you thought about things. I know I ran the house strictly and tough because I wanted you to make the most of your chance in this country. I didn't understand you as American kids."

That was the first time he'd ever said that.

My brother and I looked at him and said, "Maybe as kids, we didn't understand. We fought you because we were American teenagers who wanted the brand-name clothes and things you couldn't give us. But that's not what mattered. What you gave us was far more valuable: hard work, resilience, and the determination to fight through adversity. You taught us never to give up, and that lesson has been worth everything."

My dad has been overshadowed for so long because he has always focused everything on us. From our well-being and education to our own families, he has never allowed us to put him in the spotlight. His number one priority was always us. He didn't like the attention or needed any praise; he just wanted us to be happy. I wouldn't be the man I am today without him. I didn't write this book to be rich or famous; I wrote it to honor God but also to acknowledge my dad for all he has done. This was overdue. I wrote this to also honor my dad. *"We did it, Dad."* We built our version of the American Dream—it wasn't traditional, but we made it. My brother and I built this dream on your investment, your sweat and tears, and your sacrifices for us. I honor you with this book. I'm proud to be your son, and I'm proud to be Vietnamese American—something I may never have said before. Thank you for being persistent and consistent in our lives. You should be proud of what you've done. You raised two American boys who served their country proudly. We got our fighting spirit from you.

In my early twenties, I worked under an amazing woman who started as my "boss" but became more like a big sister— and after much reflection, I realized she was my work mom. I worked for her as a Loss Prevention Agent at Macy's, where I spent most of my twenties before enlisting in the Army. Andrea Borges—or "Dre"—was much more than a manager; she was my first true leader. Stern yet nurturing, she gave me invaluable life perspective. She filled a void in my heart as I navigated personal struggles, listening to me and filling those moments with her smile, laughter, and perspective. With Dre, I felt comfortable enough to pour out my heart about every heartbreak, and she built a family at work I could lean on when I felt lost. Dre lifted me up when I was tearing myself down over wrong decisions, always guiding me to focus on growth. She didn't let me impress her with words; I had to earn things through hard work. Nothing was given—she made sure that achieving something truly meant something.

Mama Dre was patient as I tried to figure out what I wanted to do with my life. I had once told her I was thinking of enlisting, and she simply asked me, "Why?" I didn't know how to answer, and honestly, I didn't like that she'd asked. Mama Dre could see I wasn't ready, and she kept me close until she thought I was. "Your heart's not in the right place," she'd say. "You shouldn't go." She was right. But years later, I betrayed that trust by enlisting without telling her. I knew this time why I needed to go, but I never said a word, worried she'd be disappointed. She found out from someone else, which I know hurt her. It felt like I'd been hiding it from her, though that was never my intention—I had my reasons.

I was going to tell her; I just didn't know how. Dre meant so much to me that I couldn't find the words to say it was time for me to leave the "nest." After I left, we'd talk now and then as the years went by. We recently lost Mama Dre to cancer. To her, I want to say that she was the foundation of my leadership. Thank you for being there, for guiding me, for believing in me when I was young and lost. I'm sorry I never got to say goodbye, but when these words reach the universe, I hope you're proud. I've become a stronger, more considerate person and have dedicated my life to helping others, as you did for me. You had a helping hand in raising me, and I want the world to know that. I love you, Mama Dre. You were a pillar in my life when I felt I had nowhere to safely lean on. I will always be grateful for you being that motherly voice I needed to grow up. I hate saying "goodbye," so this is just "a hui hou" (Hawaiian for "I'll see you later").

If you know me, you know how proud I am of the only division and unit I ever had the honor of serving with in the Army. The brotherhood and camaraderie with these men are eternal; there's nothing like it. We've endured some of the hardest times together, and I'm only alive because these men saved me on the battlefield. To my brothers of the 10th Mountain Division, 2nd Battalion, 22nd Infantry (Triple Deuce), Anvil Company 1st Platoon (and 2nd and 3rd as well, I love you all too)—if it weren't for your swift actions on Mother's Day 2008 on the objective, I wouldn't be here to write this book or celebrate any of my achievements. These men are fearless in the face of adversity. They don't talk much; they let their actions speak. They taught me courage. I'm honored to call you my brothers, knowing you're always there for me, no matter the time or distance. They don't concern themselves with your feelings; the mission always comes first, and if you hurt one of us—well, good luck.

To Weapon Squad, you bunch of delinquents—there's never been a group of misfits I love more. I'm proud of you all. We were underestimated, overlooked, and tested countless times, but we always stuck together and made it through. To Doc Williams and MSG E. Campos, I will forever be in your debt for taking care of me that night.

CSM K. Burris, I want to personally thank you. You were our third platoon sergeant in a year, tough but fair, and your relentless training and preparation kept us ready for anything. Thank you for seeing my potential and for all the opportunities and training you offered me to grow as a soldier—UAV, Combat

Lifesaver School, Military EMT. Thank you for giving me the chance to prove myself and for always encouraging me to be better. I always enjoyed hearing your conversations with God. And thank you for keeping SSG B. Hatfield, SSG R. Lopez, SFC J. Sholts, and CSM O'Keefe out of my workspaces. Order and neatness, right? All jokes aside, thank you for your leadership and belief in me. It was an honor to serve under your command.

If you brothers ever need me, I'm here. You helped me grow, not only as a soldier but as a man, helping me see the meaning of life. You've all changed my perspective, helping me learn to fight through every moment. I can't thank you all enough for that. To all my other buddies I haven't mentioned—I love you too, my brothers. I'm proud of all of you. You are my "War Tribe" (wink to SSG B. Ostos). Our Battalion symbol was three deuce cards missing the deuces of heart: "No heart, No mercy." We live by one motto: "DEEDS NOT WORDS." You all will always be my heroes. (Please forgive any ranks I may have remembered incorrectly.)

I can't mention the Triple Deuce without talking about my brother for life, Captain Clayton Hinchman. Words can't capture how much I admire you—the term "leader" is too small for your greatness. We've gone through dark times together, and we're here. We are survivors, not victims, and you refuse to let anyone say otherwise. Thank you for being my "ride or die" and accepting my imperfections. We may not be blood, but you'll always be my family, and it is my honor to call you my brother.

Thank you for choosing me to be your RTO, even though I know I fought it at times. You always believed in me, and I want you to know how much I appreciate that. I remember opening my eyes after the explosion, calling out for you because it was my responsibility to protect you. I hope I didn't let you down.

Our fate brought us together, and I don't regret any of it. "No" and "never" are not in your vocabulary; to you, challenges are just walls to tear down and conquer. You taught me that. It's one of my greatest honors to have you in my corner as a friend, family, and role model. You have made me a better leader. You're one of my favorite people to share laughter and dumb comments with. Thank you for accepting me into your life and family. Rangers lead the way, Sir! I'd follow you into battle anywhere, anytime. I salute you, brother.

Lastly, I want to honor two gentlemen I met while recovering at Walter Reed Medical Center. First, thank you to Mr. Mike Conklin for supporting my transition from the military by providing career and financial support. It's tough for veterans to trust many nonprofits that often take advantage of people in recovery, but Sentinels of Freedom was different. Actually, Mr. Conklin and I ended up interviewing each other, and I wasn't initially under consideration until Mr. Marty Kaplan, one of the advisors, mediated. I know I'm a bit of a handful, but I'm grateful I was accepted. Sentinels of Freedom is a first-class organization, and Mr. Conklin, you are a man of your word. Thank you for changing my life and for all you've done for our veteran community after raising three Army Rangers. I salute you and thank you for giving me an opportunity to prove myself..

Mr. Bob Nilsson—my advisor, mentor, and one of my top five Marines. A true man of service, even beyond his years in uniform, you saw something in me from the beginning. I remember you telling me as I left WRMC that I would be an entrepreneur and that you'd always be there for me. You've stayed true to those words, "Devil Dog," and everything I've done in the construction industry has been possible because of your belief in me. I'm honored to have crossed paths with you. Thank you for everything. Bob, a retired Marine and construction executive, is also the founder of 100 Entrepreneurs and, at eighty-something, has more energy than a twenty-year-old. You are one hell of a legacy, Bob. He's helped over a hundred veteran-owned companies. This Marine doesn't stop, and I love you for that. I'm forever grateful for you, Bob, more than words can express. You always knew… Semper fi, Sir!

I sit on the Board of Directors for both these organizations because I am an alumnus of both programs. These are "deeds, not words" organizations that are true to their causes. If you would like to learn more about them and support them, please check out the following links:

- **Sentinel of Freedom:** www.sentinelsoffreedom.org
- **100 Entrepreneurs:** www.100entrepreneurs.org

I want to dedicate a song to this chapter: "Lean on Me" by Bill Withers:

"Lean on me when you're not strong,
and I'll be your friend.
I'll help you carry on.
Please swallow your pride,
for no one can fill those of your needs
that you won't let show.
You can call on me, brother,
when you need a hand;
we all need somebody to lean on."

I did not make it this far in life by myself. I have been blessed with those who saw my potential and had their belief in me. I've always felt that I have had "angels' in my life guiding me through this journey... I know it's not coincidental. His grace and love are a blessing to allow such great people to support me through all of it.

CHAPTER 8

"Father God, I am just learning how to pray; bear with me.
First, I thank you for the life of everyone that's here with me,
then I thank you for the love you gave me..."
–DMX, "The Prayer IV"

This is my self-reflection, and as you've read, I am not a perfect person—I still have more of my journey to go. It's taken a long time to reach this point, but I wouldn't change anything. The lessons I've learned are too valuable to trade for something else. Everything I've done in my life has made me who I am today. My perspective has changed. There's a great quote from entertainer Pitbull: "There is no such thing as failure. You either win, or you learn." I'm too old and tired to run anymore, but now, I'm a fighter. I'm okay with facing myself and understanding what I need to get through it. As they say, "F around and find out." I live with my own expectations, under-standing my limitations, but I also know I'm willing to break through my boundaries and face the next challenge. I'm not entitled to anything.

I hope that as you read this, you understand that I am not a victim in any way. I am accountable for my decisions and for any lack of understanding that has put me in difficult situations. When I talk about others' expectations weighing on me, it's because I allowed that to happen. I didn't stand up for myself because I didn't know who I was. I didn't have faith in myself or in God to guide me. I can't look at others and ask why my life isn't like theirs; that would make me ungrateful, and I've already been blessed with a beautiful and interesting life. There came a moment when I had to realize that no one else could help or push me through—only I could do that for myself.

Live by the decisions you make, be accountable for them, and know that sometimes they won't be good, but learn from them. There's a reason you made each choice, good or bad, so be gracious with yourself because I know I wasn't. When people read this book, they'll realize I've been beating myself up for years, but with God, I've been able to understand my process and move forward.

Life moves too fast to waste time on self-pity—take it from me. The best thing I did was roll up my sleeves, face myself in the mirror, and be honest with myself. Better late than never. It's either slay or be slayed, but know that you're responsible for your own victories. So take the time to be accountable first; that's yours to own. That conversation with yourself becomes much easier when you're consistent about being true to yourself. Stop looking elsewhere and comparing yourself to others, trying to get where they're going. You have your own journey to take, and be willing to put in the work—that's the important part of all this. We keep trying to reach others' endpoints without focusing on our own.

With this "borrowed time," I regret nothing. There's no time in this life to stand around looking back. That's part of why I share my experiences in this book for others to see. Good or bad, those things are already done. Remorse is one thing, but regret is just a lack of ownership over what happened, or it did not go the way you planned it to go. There is no "should have" or "could have"—those are just entertaining conversations. Learn to accept it. People love asking if I regret joining the Army now that they know I was injured on duty. Who am I supposed to be mad at, or who could I blame? I'd do it all over again and not change a thing. I only get frustrated sometimes because adapting to change can be hard, and it's difficult to see your "new" potential when you haven't figured it all out yet. But I know I will—God will help me through that. I trust Him. He has guided me through some of these conversations and helped me understand what I need to focus on. Sometimes, it's just a shift in perspective—a single degree that opens up new possibilities. That's how I've learned to be gracious with myself.

I don't believe in doing things just for the sake of doing them anymore. Everything has to be intentional, even through the chaos. I always try to consider the impact my actions may have on myself and others. That consideration helps me in my conversations with God. God brings peace and clarity to my life. My belief in God is strong now because I've stopped asking questions that don't help me grow or see the world with light. I'm not ignoring things; I'm simply not focusing on what I can't control. Now and then, I slip because I'm human. But I know I'm here for a reason. This opportunity at life must bring meaning and connection to those I interact with. I must be intentional because time is on no one's side, so why waste it?

Learning to love yourself and knowing how to love yourself are crucial because that enables you to build, limit, and grow other relationships. I've learned to appreciate the small things and gestures, not the grand ones. The genuineness behind those things matters, and knowing the intent is important.

As a young man, even as a kid, I hated being the underdog—but I think I hated being underestimated even more. I can tell you now, though, that I appreciate being the underdog. There's an advantage in operating under the radar, free from the pressure of others' expectations, and keeping your abilities close to your chest. When people underestimate you, they don't understand your capabilities, and you get to surprise them. Embrace that—it builds character and grit.

Believe in yourself and defy what others say or think about you. It doesn't even matter what they think; you know your value, and God knows your value. Personal growth depends on how you handle adversity and the time you take to reflect and understand it. It's all part of the process. I've stopped apologizing, too. There's a difference between taking accountability and simply apologizing. In society, we often use apologies to make up for a lack of accountability, and it's weakened their meaning and sincerity.

I didn't write this book to tell you that I "made it." As I said earlier, I didn't want to write about my accomplishments without sharing the struggles I went through to get here. I truly don't believe that accomplishment defines who you are. For me, it will always be about the journey. The journey explains and develops your character and what you went through... the end result is a short glimpse of where you made it to. I'm sharing this in the hope that it might impact you if you need it. You're not alone. If you've ever felt lost, like the only person standing in a crowded room, consider this my olive branch to you—you don't have to walk this journey by yourself.

Define your success and what it means to you, then figure out how to get there. Success isn't something to talk about; it's meant to be seen through your confidence in what you've done and who you've become. It belongs to you and the values you set for it. Expect and prepare for the lows so you can fully enjoy the highs. Success comes in seasons. Like trees, we go through cycles: rebirth in spring, peak in summer, and hibernation in winter. These cycles make us stronger and deeper-rooted. With every up and down, every lesson learned, you become a stronger version of yourself.

I've chosen to see life from a different perspective now—it's almost like I'm working on my own obituary. I ask myself every day, *If I died today, what would people say about me?* That question started my journey. What have I done to create impact? Did I do what God sent me to do? I'm on this journey for God and my family; they are my legacy. My imprints on this world should be based on my actions, decisions, and contributions to making this world a better place. It's not about me anymore; I'm just grateful to be part of this. I want to appreciate what I have. Legacy isn't about being remembered—it's about planting seeds of kindness and love, living on in the hearts of others.

I believe in paying it forward. It's a beautiful way to live—doing something for someone with the hope they'll do something for another person. I've seen the darker side of life, where lives are reduced to numbers, but I've also witnessed the amazing part, where we come together as a community to achieve something greater than ourselves.

I'm not here to change who you are, but I hope that by reading this, you understand that we're all on "borrowed time." What you do now for yourself matters. You're not alone. It may feel tough right now, but I promise you, this too shall pass. We just have to keep our heads up, focus on the road ahead, and take one step at a time. Accept your faith and fate, but define your destiny.

CONCLUSION

"The 3 C's of Life: Choices, Chances, Changes —
*You must take a **choice**, to take a **chance**,*
*or your life will never **change**."*
–Naina Sanghvi

I have thanked many people in this book, but I haven't taken the time to thank my Lord, "The Father, The Son, and the Holy Spirit." When I was lost, You were always there to guide me. When I gave up on this world and myself, You lifted me up and walked with me. When I thought I was taking my last breath, You gave me life and hope. When I hid to weep, You sent Your angels to embrace me. You are the compass in my heart. Thank You for believing in me and finding value in me when I couldn't find it in myself. I am forever grateful for this time and will continue to serve You faithfully. I am a spiritual person, not necessarily religious, but You know where I stand with You. I will always trust You, my Lord. I will forever be Your soldier, ready to fight in Your honor.

We've discussed perspectives in this book, but not how others might perceive me. I believe this book may surprise people with the vulnerability I've shared. I've never discussed some of these experiences outside of those who shared them with me. This is the main point I want to convey: People may think they know you, but they rarely know your full story. Those who do know me have walked with me without judgment, and I can't thank them enough for letting me be myself. I mentioned earlier it's often those who smile, who take care of others, who remain calm through the chaos and put others first —who checks on them? We rarely know what's going on inside or the history they carry. I'm not implying that something is wrong with everyone, but we often don't know the journey that's shaped the person standing before us. So, let's be kind, graceful, and compassionate with each other. This world is hard enough; we don't need more judgment. Slow down, embrace the appreciation for what we have, and connect with those who matter to us.

To my readers, thank you for coming on this journey with me. Thank you for allowing me to build this connection. You could have spent your time elsewhere, but you made it to the end of this book, and I want you to know how much I appreciate you. When all is said and done, perceptions and expectations from others won't matter. I hope you're happy with the person you are, and I hope I've planted a seed of impact within you to keep fighting and keep moving forward. You matter. We're all just human beings walking our own paths, searching for meaning.

To my amazing father, *We did it, Dad.* We built this American Dream together, and I couldn't have done it without you and all your sacrifices. This isn't just for me; it's a recognition of the challenges you faced, standing by as I stumbled and got back up. I know it was painful for you to watch, but thank you for letting me become my own man and for allowing me to learn life's lessons. I know if it were up to you, you'd have saved me every time. I always knew you were there, my guiding light. Thank you, and I love you, Dad.

There comes a moment when you have to say goodbye, but it has to be on your terms. It is not always ideal, but if I could... I would try. It is very difficult to say farewell for me, but it must be done. If I had any second thoughts about my life, it's that I've always felt one part was incomplete. The Army gave me a purpose to serve others, a command I received from God. I fell short of completing that objective—Sgt. Timothy Van Orman never made it home to his family. I take it personally, not as a martyr or a hero, but because I believed deeply in the mission. I won't forget it, but I need to forgive myself. I don't miss the Army itself; I miss the brothers I served with, and I wonder what I could have accomplished had things gone differently. I know I didn't fail, but I still need my own closure. Sgt. Van Orman, you'll always be my ideal. Thank you for the impact and life lessons you've taught me. You're always in my heart, and now, I'm ready to close this chapter on my own terms.

"Anvil 1-7, Anvil 1-7... this is Anvil 1-6-Romeo. This is my last radio transmission. Please tell my 1st Platoon brothers that I love them. Thank you for always having my back and believing in me. I'm sorry that I didn't get to finish the mission with you guys, and that I never got to say goodbye. I would have loved to end my career with you all, but life doesn't always give us what we want—only what we need. I

will always have your six, and I promise not to waste this borrowed time, to always try to create impact where I can. I want you to be proud of me. Oh, and Anvil 1-7… tell the boys to keep their sh*t organized, I won't be around anymore to keep them in line. Anvil 1-6, you are my brother for life, I love you man. You lead and I will follow. Take care, gentlemen. It was my honor to have served with you. I salute you all."

- *Anvil 1-6 R out. -*

The journey starts and continues with you.

"LEAD WITH COURAGE!" & "DEEDS NOT WORDS."
–2nd Battalion 22nd Infantry Regiment
Anvil Company 1st Platoon

Respectfully,
Sgt. Tran, HT (retired)

THANK YOU FOR READING MY BOOK!

Just to say thanks for buying and reading my book,
I would like to connect!

Scan the QR Code Here:

SCAN ME

I appreciate your interest in my book and value your feedback as it
helps me improve future versions of this book. I would
appreciate it if you could leave your invaluable review
on Amazon.com with your feedback.
Thank you!

Made in United States
Orlando, FL
19 March 2025

59629216R00090